IT'S IN YOUR DREAMS

A SPIRITUAL JOURNEY TO RECLAIM A LIFE WORTH LIVING
WILDERNESS, ADVENTURE, AND A SPIRITUAL QUEST
TO HEAL FROM LYME DISEASE

JACLYN SANIPASS

ISBN: 978-1-7349819-0-2 (paperback)
ISBN: 978-1-7349819-1-9 (hardcover)

Cover design by 100Covers
Interior design by FormattedBooks

This book is dedicated
to the new earth

"You can have the pot of gold
at the end of the rainbow,
you just have to walk to get it."

David Lonebear Sanipass

Table of Contents

Introduction ix

1. My Early Connection With The Wild 1
2. Running..7
3. Undecided, Undeclared 12
4. There Has to Be More to Life than This 15
5. The Promise of the West..30
6. Finding Myself in The Desert Southwest......................35
7. Committed to the Path..56
8. Pizza Pinwheels and the Backcountry 68
9. Finding My Teacher 75
10. Entering the "Real" World 78
11. To Florida..80
12. To Tucson..84
13. Colorful Colorado & The High Desert.........................91
14. Seeking Treasure on the Mountain............................94
15. The Instructor Course..100
16. Solo 112
17. Living the Dream 117
18. The Crossroads 122
19. Confusion & the Pressure to Give 110% 126

20. Death or Dream?...131

21. The Crow In My Closet..135

22. The Dreaded Diagnosis 137

23. Early Diagnosis and the ER..139

24. "Post-Lyme Syndrome" A True Quest For Healing...........145

25. Seeking Help Out of State 147

26. Invisible Illness 149

27. A Speck of Light 154

28. The Cave of Despair...156

29. The Voice...160

30. A Spark of Hope and Healing 166

31. Old Turtle and the Earth Lodge 174

32. Following the Signposts on the Path 177

33. Energy Medicine & The Wilderness 187

34. The Miracles on the Path to Peru 194

35. The Hope of Destiny 202

36. The Invitation to TEA'S..206

37. Three Days Out...211

38. Remembering the Earth's Vibration..................................217

39. A New Way to Experience the Earth 220

40. To Go Beyond..229

41. Thoughts on Healing 231

Acknowledgments...233

About the Author 235

Can You Help? 237

Next Steps...239

Introduction

In 2006, I went from living my dreams guiding wilderness expeditions in the high mountains to living my nightmare in just a matter of a few weeks. What would you do if your life suddenly changed? Having Lyme disease greatly shifted my path and my world around me. It was traumatic, emotional, frightening, and frustrating. It brought me to my knees, literally. But it also brought me to places I had never imagined before and to deep meaningful connections with people I never would have met otherwise.

This story is being shared, not only to give hope to anyone struggling with Lyme disease or an unknown illness, but also for those of you who want to dream up a better future for yourselves, your family, and the world.

Do you ever feel like you're so down or in so much of a hole you can't get out? Or you are stuck in a cycle and can't break free?

In this story I share my real life experiences from the very bottom—being bed-ridden with an illness with no known cure, with no hope. Through adventurous storytelling, I share the thoughts and actions that got me through that horrendous experience and back on track to living an amazing life.

I want to show you that anything is possible. That secret to your happiness is in your dreams. You already have it, you have the secrets, you just might need to dig a little to find it. Join me on this journey and please enjoy these spiritual and life changing adventures...

1. My Early Connection With The Wild

I wasn't interested in Barbie dolls or dress-up, I was more interested in digging my bare hands into the damp, dark earth, picking up clumps of grass and muck, and spreading it over my bare skin. I'd lay on the back lawn looking up at the sky, the grass tickling my bare skin, and I'd bake in the sun. The color of the mud would fade from deep brown to light gray. As it dried, the mud would shrink, crack, and tug at the tiny hairs on my arms making my skin itch before finally flaking off.

I worked myself deeper into the earth and the elements focusing on my breath and how the sound changed when I lay closer to the earth. I could feel my pulse, my heart beating a low rhythmic thudding interrupted by the high-pitched sound of a mosquito's buzz in my ear. My concentration was only broken by the call of an osprey hovering, fishing the river nearby.

The breeze would blow gently over my skin and I'd lose my thoughts in the swooshing sound of the pine needles until the screen door would creek open a crack, my mom would poke her head out, and I'd hear, "Jaclyn!" signaling it was either time for dinner, or time for bed.

Having the freedom to roam and explore the land was a precious gift given to me by my parents. Even as a young girl, being on the water or in the forest would fill me with a deep buzz of aliveness that made my body tingle. I felt such a strong connection to the earth and very "at home" in nature, and my parents nurtured that by taking me camping and canoeing before I could even walk.

Our home was a cozy cape-style house situated on the corner where two streets came together. There was a dirt path that the locals would sometimes use that ran between our yard and a large open field. The path followed a small stream that emptied into a wet area that we called "the swamp." In our backyard grew tall white pine trees with thick, rough bark quite a contrast from the sweet smell of the wild roses that had overcome part of our yard.

The pine grove in the back yard had become a place of solace for me. I'd lose myself in climbing the trees, swinging from their branches, and building forts with the earth's elements. Placing dry, fallen branches against the tree trunk added strength to the biggest fort under the largest pine. This lean-to type structure created a cave-like dwelling which became a cocoon for me to enter a new world. Sitting nestled against an old pine, feeling the rough bark on my skin, my hair riddled with sticks and debris, I'd sit comfortably in the quiet stillness. Completely absorbed in this little world, I'd dive deep into my imagination.

Sometimes I'd venture across my back yard and over the stream, looking back at our house feeling a freedom I can't explain. No one would dare to follow me out there to the grove of trees in the field beyond the stream. To me, this was the most magnificent place on earth. Climbing the tall pines I could see to the end of the street one way, and to what seemed like an endless wilderness on all sides. Seeing a fox-kill below, I would wonder what had happened here before I arrived. This was a place to sit and to dream. To listen to the trickle of the tiny stream flowing, to listen to the wind as it ruffled and shook the fresh needles of the pines. The sound soothed me as the sun filled me with a deep nostalgic warmth like being rocked to sleep in my mother's arms.

I absolutely loved having nature around me. When my mom would announce to us we were going camping, I'd be so elated. It was such a treat when our family went on adventures to explore the world beyond our backyard! I remember those road trips very well. My whole family would all pile into my dad's truck. My sisters and I would sit facing backward on a folded baby crib mattress in the back of the truck. The mattress, covered with an old Holly Hobbie crib sheet, would cushion the abrupt landing of the bumpy ride. I can still remember that queasy feeling from the bumpy roads. We would fly up off our seats and land back down with a crash. Our laughs and giggles became amplified with each bump in the road. "The bear sat around with his foot on the ground, oh the bear..." My older sister would sing between bumps and giggles as she went through all the camp songs she knew, helping us to pass the time.

Looking out the windows from the small gray Mazda pickup, the trees zoomed by the window. The single oaks, birches, and evergreens would turn into a blur. We would hear a knock on the window and turn to see Mom with a big smile waving back at us from the front of the truck sharing red shoelace licorice with Dad. Her mouth would move, "Would you like some?"

She would ask although we couldn't hear through the glass and would have to wait until we stopped to grab a handful of candy.

Behind us we pulled a 1978 pop-up StarCraft camper with a 16-foot wooden canoe resting on its roof. A red cloth was hung from the stern, waving gently back and forth to caution other drivers of its length. The beautiful Redwood Strip canoe was entirely hand built by my Dad. Seeing it trailing behind us, I remember dreaming of where we would paddle and how many loons we would see.

The truck would slow as we entered the campground. The camper and canoe bounced over the roots on the rough camp road. Once at the site, we would jump out excitedly so Mom could guide Dad while he backed the camper into the flattest and most perfect place. I can still remember the unique sound of the crank as Dad opened the pop-up making it official—we were camping.

My sisters and I spent hours in the cool lake, splashing and making up songs until way after sunset. Staying up late, we would gaze into the campfire looking for familiar shapes and symbols made by the flames and the coals. The only sounds we heard were from nearby campers and the crackle and hiss of the wood burning in the fire pit.

Later in the evening, after cooking marshmallows on the fire, we would curl up in our sleeping bags inside the pop-up. I remember how the smells of nature mixed with the musty smell of the camper. I'd scan the brown and off-white birch trees on the wallpaper looking at the tiny details as I listened to the murmur of my parents' voices and laughter until I drifted off to sleep.

The smell of the Coleman stove and sizzle of bacon would wake me in the morning. I would roll off my bed and get my feet on the cool sandy floor before untying the old rope that held the door closed. When it popped opened, I'd peek my head out of the door to see my mom tending to the tinfoil-wrapped stones glittering with the reflection from the morning sun. She would set a heavy stone on the English muffin, pressing it flat on the griddle, giving breakfast that warm, buttery, crispy grilled camping flavor.

My parents took me camping and canoeing before I can even remember. Even before I was born, my dad made a tiny canoe paddle and had it waiting for me. This small paddle matched the bigger paddles that went with his hand crafted canoe. There was a bend in the middle, as if it were a racing paddle, yet it was small enough for me to handle as a 2-year-old. I spent much of my time in the canoe in my early years on the rivers and lakes with my family. What a gift to begin life this way.

I loved the smell of the canoe and the many adventures we took. From the Northern Lakes to the Royal River in my hometown, we moved quietly over the waters. The painted turtles slipped into the river from their posts on exposed branches as we passed. The sunlight danced off the surface of the water, disguising a deer as it approached to take a drink from the water's edge. Hiding quietly, the blue heron in its stillness would blend with the tall grasses that grew up next to the banks of the river, only moving to snatch a fish—all seen from the perspective of a child's eyes over the edge of the canoe.

I wasn't aware when I was young and experiencing these adventures that those trips would change over the years and those memories would fade over time. Now what remains is just the sliver of a moment that each family member retained. It seems the only moments that were emotionally charged were the ones that stuck. We as a family remember the happy, the sad, the scary, and the funny moments. Each with our own experience of the moment, remembered by sharing our stories over homemade pizza or flipping through the photo albums that capture some of those precious moments frozen in those times on film.

2. Running

A 2-year-old with a round belly and wide curious eyes watched as Dad tied his running shoes. He stretched, warmed up, and headed down the dirt driveway toward the pavement and was off for a run. I would see him leave, and wanted to follow. At the age of 2, I knew I was capable of doing anything, so why would he leave me behind?

I began my running "career" in the diaper derbies at the local Clam Festival. My parents, one on each side of the roped off square on the library lawn, bribed me with Reese's Peanut Butter Cups to motivate me to crawl across the grass to the other side. People were gathered around all edges of the roped off area, as children in diapers went in all directions, and some just sat looking wide-eyed at everyone. Eventually I would run that distance for the peanut butter cup, and then I kept going. My mother said that I never walked, I just started out running and never stopped!

For the first three years of my life we lived in a 19th century apartment building on Bridge Street in Yarmouth, Maine. Both sets of grandparents lived next door, my great-grandmother across the street, and many of my aunts, uncles, and relatives lived on that same street. I was fortunate to have such a big, close family. They were supportive of everything we did. It was when we lived here on Bridge Street that I began running.

One fall day just after my third birthday, I ran my first "1.1-mile Fun Run." The autumn air was cool, and I was doing my favorite thing, running with Dad. People all along the course cheered me on. As I ran, my braids bounced on my shoulders. My new running sneakers glided through the damp grass and onto the dirt track where an interesting puddle caught my attention. Everyone watching clapped and yelled, encouraging me to continue to the finish line. My cousin Wendy and my older sister Lisa were behind me, cheering for me to keep going. I didn't understand the whole finish line thing at that time. Dad and I were running, it was fun, and that is all I knew. Eventually I shrugged off the puddle, and we crossed the finish line together, the first of many to come.

Everyone was so excited for me! I received a plaque for being the youngest runner in the race, it was the first award I remember receiving. My mom described me as "so proud" of my accomplishment. The plaque was a small, dark brown square wood block with brass metal adornments. One of the brass circles was decorated with a runner and the other brass tag stated that the award was for the youngest runner and gave the date. That plaque went everywhere I went. It was tucked under my pillow at night, I posed for pictures with it in front of my parent's apartment, carried it with me everywhere, and showed it to everyone at the grocery stores and around town.

From that day on, I ran as much as I could. I worked each day to run faster than before. By age four I had managed to run several road races, running with an attitude, determined to be the best I could be. I had so much fun. I loved how my ponytails swung back and forth as I ran, and my feet bounced rhythmically off the pavement. I felt so energized when people on the sidelines cheered me on, and seeing them encouraged me to go even faster.

My parents always made sure that I had good running shoes. That was the only purpose for those shoes, for running. Sitting on the ground, lacing them up was part of my ritual to prepare myself physically, emotionally, and mentally for the run ahead.

I practiced running almost every day. Over and over, I ran around the block where I lived trying to beat my best time. My younger sister would hop on her purple and white bike and I would race her on foot trying to keep up with the streamers that extended from her handlebars. If my time was slower than I wanted, I would do it again, pushing myself as hard as I could go, feeling winded, exhausted, and exhilarated by the end.

My "cross training" involved riding my pink Huffy behind my dad as he ran in front of me for many miles. I focused on staying right behind him, sometimes too close and my front tire would bump his foot. My whole family attended road races on the weekends from spring through fall. My uncle and aunt (my dad's sister and brother) both ran, as well as my cousin Wendy, my older sister Lisa, and my younger sister. Mom kept us fed, watered, and dressed for the weather and conditions. My mother always braided my hair or pulled my hair back in pigtails so I could see clearly and run even faster. She made sure my knee-high striped socks matched my running shorts, that I had good running shoes, and that I peed before the race! I continued to run throughout my early life. I was pretty serious about it, always improving my times, having fun, and trying to beat the boys in The Royal River Ramblers, our local running team.

As I grew older, I ran more races and even won a few. However I was often afraid to be out ahead in the front. I was afraid I would lose my way, even though the courses were usually clearly marked. I'd stutter my steps holding back for a moment while fighting my inner thoughts and fears. "I can go faster," I thought, still putting on the brakes...I began to realize that it is harder to hold back than to just go ahead.

When I was around 10 years old, my parents signed me up for a road race in Freeport, Maine. With the loud bang of the starting gun the race began. I jumped out in front of the pack with a few boys. Slowly the group thinned to just me and one other boy. I stayed right behind him as the run went from the paved road into the woods. I matched his feet behind him, staying right on his heels. I was afraid to pass him because I didn't want to get lost. But his pace was just too slow, and I blew by him around a corner and watched the flaggers as they told me where to turn on the race course.

I was running at just about my max. My heart pumped, I was squeezing the air into my lungs, and moving my legs as fast as they could go. I could feel the fatigue building up and my mind kicked in: "Just keep going, give it your all." My running shorts rode up as my underwear sagged out beneath the edges. My shorts chafed the inside of my thighs, but I wasn't going to let that stop me. As I rounded the corner I could see the finish line ahead. The officials were waving orange flags with stopwatches in their hands. I gave it all I had. Sprinting ahead I crossed the finish line first and slowed to a stagger to catch my breath.

When I realized I had beat everyone in that race, even all the boys, I felt a sense of accomplishment. That really meant a lot to me, it was a really good race. I did like to win, but knowing that

I gave it "my all," having nothing left at the end was the ultimate feeling. That is the feeling that drove me to continue running races. I wasn't running to race people, but when there were others there, it helped to push me further and faster than I thought I could go.

I was always trying to beat my best time, and strived to run a mile in under six minutes. Beep, beep, beep, I set the stopwatch on my wrist, this way I could see how fast I was going as I went. I had been pretty close to beating the six minute mile several times, but took to running 5Ks and dropped the idea as I got older. Each race I seemed to place well in my age group.

One fall day in northern Maine, I found myself standing in line holding a purple silk ribbon. Handing it shyly to Joan Benoit Samuelson, I felt embarrassed and upset with 7th place, but wanted the signature of my idol, this elite woman runner so bad, I was willing to endure the awkwardness. I had tripped during the start of the race, and a man behind me held me to find out if I was alright. I was yelling for him to let me go. I just wanted to race. My dad always told me that if you fall, just get up and keep going. Just get up and go and that is what I was trying to do. That slowed me down a whole minute and I was very upset!

Did you have a good time? "No, I didn't beat my time." "But did you have a good time?" "Oh yeah, I had fun." My dad always made sure that we were having fun—that was the most important thing in racing, to "have a good time." To have a "good time" meant to have fun, not beating a certain time on the race clock.

I have carried this mentality into all things in my life. I took these lessons seriously, and have implemented both messages, "if you fall, get back up and keep running, and "have fun," into everything I have done in my life since.

3. Undecided, Undeclared

When I was in third grade, only three girls played basketball, regardless I showed up every Saturday in my matching lavender colored sweatshirt, sweatpants, and my running sneakers. I dribbled and learned along with the boys in the gym, sometimes bouncing the ball off my toes and sending it across the floor to the other side of the bleachers. This experience helped me to be ok with who I was. I was very athletic and enjoyed the challenge. I practiced seriously and took every basketball class and camp I could from 3rd grade on. But basketball wasn't the only sport I got into.

In 5th grade, my friend asked me if I was going to sign up for soccer that year. Her older brothers played and we had enjoyed kicking the soccer ball around in their yard. It wasn't until I was in 5th grade when there was finally a soccer program for girls, so my parents signed me up at my request (which was more like begging to be with my friends). Little did I know soccer would become my favorite sport all the way through my senior year in highschool.

I suffered several injuries during my freshman and sophomore years in high school including a broken leg, a concussion, and a back injury, all from soccer. But my junior and senior year,

I played as hard as I possibly could and we had great teams, making it to the State Championships both years.

I enjoyed playing soccer, basketball, and softball. I also ran indoor track and raced in road races on my own. I loved competition. I loved pushing my limits and doing my best. I loved training. So when it came time to choose a college, we looked at the obvious first, perhaps getting into physical therapy. I thought it would be great to be a team doctor or a physical therapist so I could help those with injuries get back to their life and sports. I knew what it was like to be out and injured and how I relied on doctors and therapists to help get me back on the field, the court, or the trails. So I did a few internships at several physical and occupational therapy facilities during my senior year of highschool.

But while I was choosing a college, I was mostly focused on where it was located, how big or small it was, and the options for outdoor activities like hiking and camping. It was a tough choice, and the truth was that I really didn't know. I wanted to attend college very early in my life, but what for? What would I focus my studies on?

Close to the end of my senior year, I was playing in an all-star soccer tournament. It was eastern vs. western Maine with mostly seniors on the teams. As the announcers called each of us out to the field during the introductions, they would say each player's name, number, the college they would be attending, and the major they declared.

When my number was called it went more like this, "Jaclyn Ouillette, number 19, undecided and undeclared." When I heard that echo out from the big speakers on the tall poles at the corners of the announcers booth, it felt so disappointing. I wondered how everyone else knew where they wanted to go and what they wanted to do. Everyone else had schools picked and majors decided, but I had no idea. I decided after that experience (because I felt like a failure in that respect) to take a year off, work, and travel. My parents were supportive of the decisions I made.

I had been accepted to all the colleges I applied to, so it was just a matter of choice for where I wanted to go and what I wanted to study. I chose Johnson, Vermont because the school was small and located in the mountains, besides, they had a great sports medicine program. But during my year off, I spent hours and days searching and digging into what it was I wanted to do and to be in this life. I journaled, meditated, traveled, and hiked. I spent time in nature, in the woods, by the rivers, and walking along the ocean.

The year that I took off from school, the college I had chosen to attend announced a new program. They called and we talked about the new program called "Outdoor Education." I didn't even know you could go to college for outdoor education! So I signed up for the program and began in the fall.

4. There Has to Be More to Life than This

College in itself wasn't what I thought it would be. I dreamed of going away to higher education since I was young. I remember stopping while I was walking or riding my bike to pick up pennies and dimes off the ground. I'd tuck it away in my pocket thinking, "I'm going to deposit this into my college account." My dream of learning and reading big books would set me on course, I thought, to becoming really smart and successful in life. But instead, when I finally arrived, I found college to be very different than anything I imagined previously. During my first semester, I lived in a dorm room on campus with parties happening at all hours every day it seemed. There were constant distractions. Besides the living situation, the classes were very hard. Some courses I had no interest in, yet they were required for my major.

My anxiety grew and I found it hard to go to my classes. I couldn't keep up with the amount of reading and homework. I didn't even know where the computer room was until halfway through the semester, and when I found it, it was so full I'd have a panic attack just walking by the door hearing the hundreds of fingers tapping on the keyboards. I didn't know the extent of my social anxiety until that time. The way I dealt with this newly discovered anxiety was to find every swimming hole in the local area and to spend nights camping at every cabin and lean-to open for public use within 50 miles. I hiked up the creeks, hopping from rock to rock, spending entire days exploring this new "wild" in Vermont.

I failed out of every class my first semester, except for maybe receiving a D in Earth Science. It was a very hard transition for me, and feeling disappointed, I moved out of the double dorm room and into a single room for the spring semester. The experience was similar to falling, and then getting back up to run again. I felt scraped and bruised, yet determined to keep on the trail. I got back up and continued on.

I brought my sewing machine to college, so when I wasn't out exploring I was in my room sewing my own clothes to wear. I had been sewing my own clothes since high school. Soon others began to notice what I was wearing and they wanted me to sew them pants as well. Within a few weeks, I had a full time business sewing pants and embroidering patches. Students came from across campus to donate their old corduroy pants and fabrics and I sorted them all into colors and patterns. I had a rainbow of piles of fabric almost to the ceiling piled in my room and between sewing (sometimes ten hours straight) I took all of my classes over and started fresh again. I was newly inspired with creativity and that gave me the drive and energy to finish the year passing all my classes and doing very well.

Over the next few years it was up and down. The struggle to know I was in the right place was hard. I loved some of the classes and experiences, and really didn't like many of the other classes that were required. I began to party more with those around me and tried to focus more on what I found fun than what I didn't like. Stress and anxiety smoldered under the surface.

During my 3rd year in college, I lay in bed after one long night. I was alone, still in my handmade blue corduroy pants and orange long-sleeve shirt from the day before. I had been sleeping for what felt like three days. My house was empty and silent except for the running toilet and an occasional drip from the bathroom faucet just outside my bedroom door. I had locked myself in my bedroom many hours before while a wild party raged outside my door. A boyfriend I had for several years was the only one there with me in the room, yet he didn't stay too long.

The night before I had invited several friends over for a pot-luck get-together. Then the neighbors came, and their friends, and then their friends. I knew it was out of hand when I saw the layer of beer on the floor, shining and slick like a skating rink. Maybe a few weeks ago I would have thought this was fun, but my attitude had shifted. This time I was annoyed.

I asked the "guests" to turn the music down. My boyfriend at the time instigated more than helped. They had raided my fridge (what I had in there anyway) and had paid no respect to me, my words, or my apartment. So, I did the only thing I had left to do. I retreated to my bedroom, closed the door, and turned the lock, keeping everyone out. They pounded on the door and knocked on the windows, but my only response was to shut my curtains and to pull my blankets over my head. They must have grown bored when there was no more food, and eventually they were all gone, including my boyfriend, and all was quiet.

Tired of this "college lifestyle," I wanted a way out. Underneath my consistent smile and adventurous spirit, I felt used and disrespected most of the time. I tried to ignore it, but it was always there and I didn't know how to change it. I had begun to notice there was one incident after another that just didn't feel right to me. It seemed somehow that I had started to see myself and my life from an outside perspective.

Returning home after my college class one day, I found my bedroom door cracked open. This was unusual, as I usually had my door closed. When I peered through the crack I gasped as I saw my things torn apart and spread across the floor. Walking in cautiously, I looked around. "What happened?" I thought. My embroidery floss and art supplies were unravelled and scattered from my bed to the floor. What was once an emergency blanket twinkled, like tinsel thrown during a celebration. My favorite blue corduroy pants that I had made were ripped in shreds and spread across the room. Then I saw my hiking boots. My suede boots were chewed down to the soles and the straps to my back-packing backpack no longer attached. That hit me and I felt it to my core. My heart felt ripped apart that day.

I didn't care so much about the things, I knew they were just objects that could be replaced. It was a mess to clean up, but going through that experience was much deeper than just the physical objects in the physical realm. Feeling overwhelmed, something was triggered inside of me. Within the deepest part of my being, I knew my life was out of control. My life didn't feel like it was mine anymore. Somehow I landed myself in a life where I was in the starring role yet I hated the script. I wasn't happy with what I had created.

It wasn't until that moment upon awakening after the pot-luck turned wild party, when I finally acknowledged the dis-connection I felt. I acknowledged how far I was from what I had imagined my life to be. I was overcome with fear as this new realization set in...I didn't know what to do. I tried to hold my new awareness and all the feelings inside, to control it and not let it be seen. Yet it bubbled up to the surface and began to show itself to me in every situation in my life.

For instance, during the night I would awaken in a complete state of panic. It was a strange feeling because I wasn't quite awake, but I had an awareness of myself and my room. In my dream, I could see my bedroom exactly how it should be, yet I couldn't control my body. I felt I was spinning quickly, and then pushed and slammed against the walls and the ceiling. I couldn't make it back to my body, that was still sleeping in my bed. Falling suddenly, with a quick and uncontrolled heavi-ness, I'd jump and awaken sweating and gasping for air. Afraid. "What was that? What is that force?" I kept moving my bed to see if it would help but the episodes continued. I had enough.

The mountains outside my window called me to the next phase in life, yet the next day I was no closer to that trailhead. "I'm going to climb that mountain tomorrow," I kept promising myself. Then tomorrow came and went. "I will climb that moun-tain tomorrow." And that day to hike that mountain still has not arrived. I had become distracted by new and wild adventures. The swimming holes kept me afloat, yet I wasn't climbing the mountains of my dreams. I was chasing the boredom and run-ning from the gnawing fear in my life. The fear that I wasn't doing the right thing, or there would never be more to life than this.

I woke up one bright spring morning soon after to the sun shining through my window illuminating the fresh Easter lilies on the windowsill while a dog ran around my room. My head was pounding from the night before. It takes making a decision over and over again to make a change, and I had not made that change yet. "Who's dog is this?" I wondered, my thoughts spilling out of my mouth. There was a big bag of dog food and a silver dish. Turns out the dog was left with me to care for.

Laying in bed that morning, disgusted with the life I was living, my thoughts circled. In the midst of the fog, something popped into my mind, "There must be more to life than this." Again I heard that thought, "There must be more to life than this."

I was stuck. I couldn't believe it, but I had allowed myself to fall into the trap. I was chasing my dream of becoming a Wilderness Guide and my dream of working as an outdoor teacher and leader. But I got caught up in college classes, home-work, and chasing elusive knowledge. All while in the illusion of "living on the edge" with these "party animals" surrounding me in all directions. "And I created this?"

My voice was a weak whisper, yet it echoed through the empty rooms of my house. "Please help me." Three simple words that when uttered, changed the course of my life. At the same moment my frail voice escaped my mouth, a spark of light appeared in front of me and a feeling that something, perhaps an angel was there beside me. With that spark of light, I knew I had been heard.

I had to do the hard thing right then and there, to kick a boy-friend out of my home and my life. It was a long time coming, but what had stopped me? Was I so asleep that I didn't see it?

Was I so afraid that I chose not to look? Whatever it was, I am glad I woke from the nightmare. A new sense of freedom was sparked in my life that day as he headed off down the road, dragging his baggage and drama with him.

Letting go was hard as I didn't know what lay ahead of me, yet all I could do was look for change. It is always hard to lose a friend no matter the situation and circumstance. Yet as time went on, this change allowed space, and allowed more friends to come in. This opened me up to much more learning and many more adventures that I wouldn't have had access to before. My appreciation for life began to grow.

I began to allow my beliefs to come forward into the actions of my life choices. I did believe deep inside of me somewhere that there was much more to life and way more that I couldn't yet see. I discovered within the vastness of myself an idea that a different future would unfold if I took a new direction. After that moment of clarity, more magic appeared in my life, or maybe I just opened to recognize it more. I moved from my apartment, giving everything I owned, which wasn't much, away.

I was grateful for that dog becoming part of my life because he gave me something that changed me forever. I had to focus on something other than myself. I made sure to feed him and ensure that he was able to run and play. In giving this to him, I gave the same to myself as well. We bonded and had many adventures in the short time we were together. But that dog, Snoop, gave me the greatest teachings and gifts of my life. That dog taught me to get out and have fun, and to care for myself again.

My new friends and I began traveling and digging for crystals and mineral specimens. We researched crystal growth formations day and night, constantly reading and discussing our discoveries. We traveled to locations where we could have hands-on experience with the minerals and rocks of the earth.

Looking for indicator minerals, we scoured the landscape. Digging smokey quartz and amazonite, or amethyst, became common weekend trips for me. What a different way to experience the earth and life. To have my hands in the dirt helped me to feel connected again. Learning rocks and minerals of different areas opened me up to what is just under the surface that we don't see. The colors and structures of each crystal are so unique. Formed over thousands of years, they made my life seem short and insignificant. Humbling. Before my eyes seeing them, the sunlight had never touched those crystals and minerals before. I had found a new passion, the raw beauty, the awe. There was a new spark in my life that pulled me forward to dreams I hadn't had since I was a child building forts and playing in the mud.

It was a cold Vermont day in the middle of March and we were sitting around my kitchen table. My friend had discovered a recent obsession with wire wrapping and began collecting colorful craft wire from the craft store to practice with. When I arrived home from class one afternoon, I found the items on my kitchen table wrapped in blue craft wire. I mean, my scissors, salt and pepper shakers, everything was wrapped!

We talked about crystal mining possibilities for the long weekend, and decided to take a trip to New York to the great Herkimer county. This county in New York is known for producing the clearest double terminated quartz crystals in the world. If you are a rockhound, you know Herkimers! Quartz "diamonds" from Herkimer County New York are some of the most spectacular in the Northeast. We had seen the crystals before and were absolutely amazed at their clarity. We looked in the Rockhound's Guide to New York for the mining localities of these precious beauties. There were so many stories from rockhounds that we just couldn't not experience this.

We made a simple plan and set off to find Fonda, New York. We were told that we would easily be able to find a "tall man," (no one seemed to have his name) we would each buy him a cappuccino at the gas station nearby, and in return for the cappuccinos, he would allow us to dig on his property to find "Herks." Or so that is what we thought.

We drove from Vermont in a general direction. We were looking for a place that fit with stories we heard from those who visited before. We didn't have an exact address, or name. We arrived in Fonda, New York and almost immediately were pulled over by the police. I can't remember what for, but while we were out of the car we looked down on the ground and found a beautiful perfect tiny herkimer "diamond" quartz. When my friend got back in the car, he said, "This is good. We are close to the crystals!" So at least getting pulled over gave us a positive clue that we were, in fact, in the right place. My friend always looked for the learning in each situation, and could turn anything around to be a positive experience.

Along the way, we pulled off the road onto the soft shoulder, taking a break from the drive to help us get our bearings. We were parked off the road enough to be out of the way of other cars. There was an old rock wall that followed the length of the road, so we walked along it and stretched our muscles a bit. The wind blew and the tops of the trees swayed back and forth. My friend took one of the rocks from the top of the rock wall and swung his rock hammer down, striking the center of the rock and splitting it just about evenly. As the rock broke open, splitting in two, the glitter of the reflection sparkled in the sun, "Another Herkimer diamond!" We were in the right area, there were obvious crystals. So where were the football-sized crystals we heard about?

We had no place to stay that night and thought it would be too cold to camp. So instead of getting out and setting up a tent, we stayed in the tiny white Tercel, shivering and trying to stay warm through the night. It was frigid, and snowflakes fluttered down from the dark night sky. We would turn on the car and blast the heat, then turn it off. We would warm it up and then the heat would dissipate leaving us miserably cold. We had to keep shifting to ease our sore and cramped muscles. Switching seats to "stay warm and comfortable" was the thought, however the discomfort grew until the coldest part of the morning just before sunrise. We were so happy to see the sun that morning when it began to shine! Blasting through the leaves in the trees next to us, the light began to warm the day and we were once again filled with hope for a successful adventure.

Flipping through the dog-eared and creased pages of the Rockhound's Guide to New York, we searched for the location to check out. The guidebook had been well used, probably for years before we received it as a gift. We treated it as a treasure map for our journey.

In the book we read about private property where we could mine these special Herkimer crystals. The book said to place a dollar in the mailbox, park by a wooden outhouse at the edge of the back lawn, and then dig the land behind the house. We followed just that and parked near the trail. The trail brought us into the forest through the tall trees. Within a few yards we could see the land was completely dug up. Mounds of dirt, holes deeper than me, and piles of rock exposed the human desire for these shiny crystals. We read stories that the owners discovered a football-sized Herkimer Diamond crystal when the hole was dug for the outhouse, and others had devoured the land in search of the big, shiny, clear, and rare ones. We were excited to begin and ready to find some super-shiny specimens and at the same time my heart felt heavy looking at the devastation to the land.

Dumping the small selection of hand tools out on the ground, we began to dig. I sifted through the piles that others had left behind. Most of the rock hounds were looking for the big, crystal clear ones, I loved the tiny, cute, sparkly ones. My fingers became dry and caked with dirt as I went from pile to pile sifting through to find the sparkles. Each crystal was so unique it was hard to move fast. I stopped and appreciated every glitter I saw. The Earth is absolutely amazing, and this was proof.

After a full day of digging by ourselves, a young man emerged from the woods, surprised to see us. He had been next door digging, which was obvious by the dirt all over him. He heard us, so he came over to find out what we were doing not knowing there was a dig there as well. After talking for quite a bit, we realized that we had been looking for the man who lived next door. We were so close and didn't even know! What we were looking for was right next to us all along. So we packed up our tools, headed down to the store in town. We picked up two hot cappuccinos to give as gifts.

We made our way back to the edge of town along the windy New York countryside and turned into the short dirt driveway. This "driveway" was more like a trail wide enough for a car. The parking area consisted of a few spaces amongst the trees between the roots. There were quirky signs hung at various heights on the trees. One designated a handicap parking place. There was also a white wooden sign with black letters that spelled out "Witchdoctor." There were several other signs, some crooked and some straight that read "keep out" and "private property no hunting."

We decided to park in the non-handicap spot and walked over the roots and through the woods to a tiny trailer. A ferocious white chihuahua was the first to greet us. We could hear someone inside the trailer bumbling around and saying, "Who is it? I'll be right there......I'm coming, I'm coming." There were a few more crashes and bangs before the door creaked open. A very tall man dressed in a full purple sweat suit ducked his head down and then out the door. With a smile he said, "Hello and what the hell are you doing here?" We handed him the cappuccinos and asked if we could dig for crystals. He accepted the two drinks that were now cool and invited us to come inside.

We sat inside the small trailer for two days listening to his stories. The stories went from UFOs to predicted floods, to astral projecting. We sat at a very small table in the trailer. I was uncomfortable with the small space and strange conversation. I would have left if my friend hadn't wanted to stay. He was intent on digging for "Herkimer diamonds" on that land. Once we listened long enough, the tall man allowed us into his personal pit and we began to dig. There were blue tarps set up to keep us somewhat dry as the rain had set in. We dug. Dirt filled my old work gloves as I worked with hand tools to remove the rocks. I turned each rock over to see if there were sparkles. The reflections of light are indicators of the Herkimer "diamonds."

We went on for a long time digging and finding nothing. We dug deeper, smearing dirt on our foreheads to wipe away the sweat. All while the tall man was behind us would pull out a shiny crystal saying, "Oh a beautiful gemstone, another beautiful gemstone. Every few seconds we would hear him again, "Oh what a beautiful stone, another beautiful gemstone." My friend and I kept looking at each other like what the heck? We were digging and working so hard and not finding a thing!

That night the tall man cooked us mashed potatoes and bacon. A big pot was set on top of an old kerosene heater and we took turns mixing. After the meal, he set us up in a trailer to sleep. I was a little scared we would topple over in the night. The camper was one that would be set on the back of a pickup. But there was no pickup. It was set on some poles and stacked wood. We were warmer than sleeping in the car and grateful for a good night's sleep. In the morning we had breakfast together and he shared with us more stories, many more stories.

We had asked about the Herkimer diamonds and this time he told us more. He shared how they grow in veins and how to determine the direction that the veins run to help us find them. Then he told us even more.

"A long long time ago, New York and the surrounding area was covered with oil. It was the largest oil spill of its kind. The oil had been there for a very long time and there was a certain bacteria that fed on the oil. The bacteria grew in size as it began to consume the oil. The bacteria looked like little dragons and as they fed on the oil, they grew bigger and bigger. After ingesting the oil, the bacteria would defecate double terminated crystals. At first these were microscopic, but there was so much oil to eat, the bacteria grew very large. They grew into full sized dragons.

The dragons excreted double terminated crystals and as the dragons grew, so did the crystals. The dragons kept growing until one day the oil was all gone, at which time the dragons died off. All that remains here from that time is the Herkimer diamond quartz and anthraxolite. He explained this black mineral was the remnants of the oil that had dried up. That was the first time I had ever heard of anything like that. So I asked, "So are you saying that we are mining ancient dragon poop?"

We walked around the back yard where there was more trillium than anywhere else I had ever seen. All different colors, big, lush, and thick. It was absolutely amazing. I wondered if the crystals and the crystal structure provided some perfect balance for the plants to grow and thrive. I had felt a bit sad looking at the earth and how it had been dug up. This property wasn't nearly as bad, but where we had been next door, there were pits and holes everywhere. People had come to dig for quartz, yet had stripped away everything. They were tearing apart the land to see and take the crystals. Many were there to mine and sell these rare Herkimer "diamond" crystals. And these were just the small personal pits. There were larger commercial areas nearby that were even more destroyed. I began to think more about what I was doing as we headed back to the main pit on the property.

I pulled each stone out so carefully. No crystals, just rocks and dirt over and over. Just as I was about to give up, I pulled out a stone and on the end facing away from me I saw the sparkle of light reflected from the sun. I used my bare hand to wipe away the damp earth that stuck to the rock and revealed a smooth surface and even more shine. This rock had so many tiny, glittering quartz. It was drusy quartz! I wiped away the damp dirt and revealed a very nice double terminated quartz centerpiece atop the hundreds of small ones. This was one of the most beautiful specimens I had ever seen! I felt complete with the dig and have never returned. We left that day with sparkling treasures and headed home toward Vermont. We arrived back at school feeling refreshed, revived, and ready for life's next adventures.

The excitement from this trip sparked the desire in me to always continue learning. Through experiences I could learn something new everyday. Yet, I realized that the journey is up to me. I was reminded that each day is an opportunity to create our life through seeking out new adventures, and having the courage to truly go for it.

5. The Promise of the West

looked down around me at all the things that had piled up as a voice came through the open door from the other side of the car. "Where is the piece of the map for the lower part of Arizona?" I couldn't even find my feet let alone find the atlas. So I rummaged through the piles of mismatched shoes, water bottles, coffee mugs, and clothing. "Aha here it is." I said, flipping through the torn and dog-eared atlas. I quickly discovered the page we needed was missing. It had been torn out some time ago. There was still a possibility that it was in the car somewhere, perhaps it was stuffed under the seat? Or shoved in the glove box?

We had been following hand-drawn maps on napkins and sticky, paper placemats for weeks. By following people's words and descriptions we found ourselves on a wild goose chase around the Southwest in search of crystals. We gathered many stories and slept on countless dirt roads in makeshift campsites in search of precious minerals. We stumbled upon old prospectors out in the hills who were still out there looking for gold. They shared with us stories of the first gold nugget they found 30 years ago which kept them hopeful that today would be the day they would find another. Our travels and crystal seeking brought us to a friend of a friend who lived in Tucson.

The first time I met the Tucson desert, our friends had decided to take us on a hike to explore a small cave. We brought water bottles with us, gallon jugs. It was 105 degrees outside the air-conditioned car. Making the transition from the cool car to the desert air proved difficult. We stepped carefully out into the dry dirt ground of the desert. The first step out of the car I received a blast to my face in the form of a thick wall of hot air which squeezed my lungs. It was hard to see the beauty, my eyes stinging from sweat dripping from my brow. We walked in slow motion toward the cave. It was less than a quarter mile away. I found out right then that I'm not exactly a desert girl! I did make it to the cave, and was just as happy to make it back to the car. We headed back north pretty quickly after that! Back to the mountains and cooler weather with the promise to return to the desert later that fall.

When the cooler weather came, so did the next adventure to the desert. We packed the van, several people and dogs, and headed out to an old mining town on the border of Arizona and Mexico. We found the location rather easily, parked the van and began to walk around. This had been an old mining town and still had that feeling. Some buildings still stood, although they had been abandoned for years. Many of the structures were leaning to one side or the other, with chains across the doors and boards nailed in front of the windows. It was a rather creepy ghost town. I wondered what happened here. Did everyone leave at once? In some of the mines poisonous gases escaped and the miners would have to abandon the site, or so the stories go. In some places they ran out of the metals or minerals they were mining, or ran out of money searching. I decided to stay away from the old entrances to the mines just in case. We began to dig and sift through the tailings nearby.

This location had small piles of raw chrysocolla, a beautiful green-blue mineral which looks similar to turquoise. In the dirt I found wire and old porcelain buttons. I would hold them and imagine who had been wearing that button, and what their life would have been like. They probably wouldn't even have missed this button, but it was such a curiosity to me.

As the sun set, the darkness began to creep across the land. "Ok, we gotta go before it gets too dark," came the voice of our friend, the driver, and our guide for the day. So we all loaded up in the van assuming that we would begin our way down the dirt road. Yet, with the turn of the key there was a low whining sound. The van started reluctantly and the lights were very dim...a clear sign of a low battery.

So we pushed the van down the dirt road, with all the lights off to preserve the battery hoping to make it to the next town. We were making progress when we came around a corner to meet face to face with a large cow. We had to stop to avoid hitting the stubborn animal who had no interest in moving out of our way. The two in the front hopped out and tried to wave the cow out of the road. Then they tried to push it and bribe it, but that cow was not moving! So they got back in the car and drove around and off the road… and we headed to the next town with all of the lights off in the vehicle, as well as the headlights and taillights.

By this time the sun had set and it was dark. The passengers in the front and back held flashlights to light the road as we preserved every ounce of power in hopes of making it to that town. We just came over the top of the hill when all power went out and the engine stalled. We were coasting down the hill when I saw orange sparks shoot out behind us and bounced off the road. First the van was not driving, and now I see fire! I was nervous and all of the dogs were on high alert.

We coasted to a stop at the bottom of the hill, pulled off the road in a sandy spot, and parked. We got out to assess our situation. Just then, two headlights came down the hill and slowed on it's approach. The vehicle turned in and parked right behind us. An officer stepped out of the jeep with a bright flashlight on all of us. And then came the questions. It was a Border Patrol officer. We explained our situation with the car battery. The officer gave our van a jump and set us in the direction of the next town which was a few miles up the road.

We made it up that hill, down the road and coasted into a parking space right in the center of town on the side of Main Street. We hopped out and decided to sit down for a pizza while we asked the locals for directions to the nearest Walmart. Luckily there was one open late about 12 miles away.

Full and nourished from the pizza we went outside on the sidewalk and began to ask around again for another jump. The people in the town were quite friendly and the jump came easily. The next thing we knew we were headed down the road toward Walmart. Again we just barely coasted into the parking lot on the last bit of juice from the previous jump. We took the battery out and headed into the store to the return counter. The battery must have been bad because it was new and wouldn't stay charged. They let us exchange it for another one off the shelf. After replacing the battery, the van started up with one quick turn of the key and we headed off down the road back toward Tucson.

Several months later I returned to Tucson for a semester with the National Outdoor Leadership School or NOLS for short. This would also be my very first Tucson gem show. Driving into Tucson, I didn't realize what a big and sprawling city it was. I also didn't realize that there was a Fourth Street, Fourth Avenue, Fourth Road, and so on, so we were driving back and forth for hours looking for the NOLS base. There were no GPS or smartphones at the time, and all we had was the bits and pieces left of the old atlas. We depended on the kindness of others at the gas stations and cross roads, but we had no luck finding the road we were looking for. We took advice from some folks at the gem show in town and headed up toward the hills where there was land and free camping.

We slept on the side of a dirt road, on a hill with an angle so every time I fell asleep I slid down the hill a few feet. I'd wake up, shivering from the cool night air and crawl back up the hill to settle in again. It was a rough night sleep, plus the anxiety of my new adventure ahead kept me awake and my thoughts churning. I would be spending the next 88 days living and traveling outdoors, with a group of people that I had never met before!

6. Finding Myself in The Desert Southwest

We began the semester-long course at the NOLS base, which was simply a roof over smooth concrete tucked away into the landscape at the edge of Tucson, Arizona. I lay beneath the acacia trees and the giant saguaro, resting in my newly issued sleeping bag. This was much warmer than the well-used sleeping bag with the broken zipper I had brought with me. It actually zipped and held me tight inside.

The group was excited, and everyone was on their best behavior. We were new to each other and so each of us walked delicately, being extra polite and saying, "No, thank you, that's ok." Gracefully covering up those little things that bugged us we all held those just under the surface. It is easy to let things go at first, to slip them quietly into the darkness and shadow of the subconscious mind for the sake of getting along and making new friends.

We prepared ourselves for the next few weeks in the backcountry. The first classes included learning how to pack our backpacks and cooking in the backcountry. We learned how to cook pasta and pancakes in the fry bakes on WhisperLite gas stoves. We learned about the "twiggy fire," a small fire made on the lid to bake in the backcountry, how cool! The food was going to be amazing, and for the record, this was the first place I had ever heard of quinoa. We learned wilderness first aid including backcountry care for wounds and broken bones. Through elaborate and realistic-feeling scenarios, we learned how to deal with impalements and potential evacuations, hoping to never have to use these skills.

We weighed our rations and packed our backpacks. I had brought a comfy old Lowe Alpine pack with me. This backpack was slightly smaller than recommended. But I was determined to use the one I had been practicing with, and I was willing to make sacrifices to make that happen. As somewhat of a newbie in the wilderness (even though I had car-camped my whole life) my amateur mind was in the lead. Many of the others in the group had never camped or spent a night outdoors before.

I made sacrifices and left some things behind to lighten the load and compacted everything I could. Cutting the length of my toothbrush and spoon handles was an easy fix. In the absence of that unnecessary pack weight, I found it important to insert a small cloth with tiny crystal specimens and a little green glass Buddha. Deeming them important to my purpose for this trip, I found a way to make sure they were included.

I rolled the tiny crystals in the cloth carefully each day and kept them easily accessible in the hood of my pack while we traversed the wilderness. Each night I unrolled the cloth and checked in with each piece. My mini rock collection included smoky quartz, clear quartz, amethyst, fluorite, goshenite, helidore, lemurian seed crystal, and an apatite crystal. I asked them to keep me safe while I slept. The natural facets of the crystals glittered in the light of the moon. I was convinced they would provide safety, protection, and would help open my mind and assist vivid dreams. I'm glad I never had any real run-ins with any rattlesnakes or scorpions, because the crystals probably wouldn't have helped that!

Since we were in the desert, I left my head exposed to the elements while I slept. My eyes, when opened, were facing directly up to the stars. What an experience this was. "How lucky am I to have this moment?" Although filled with the beauty and vastness of the night sky above the desert, internally I felt completely alone. Friends were out there somewhere, it was just a matter of finding them. I felt that I didn't quite belong in this group, but that was nothing new, just an idling feeling that I had carried with me most of my life.

In the morning, I tried to stuff my down sleeping bag into the bottom of my pack. It was a little extra bulky because of the elestial smokey quartz I had stored in the bottom. It added so much weight to my already-on-the-smaller-side pack! But I felt this crystal was a necessity to have with me. I felt connected and in awe when I peered into the galaxies held within this particular crystal. Although it was a charcoal gray in color, It was very clear and had a golden hue as the sun shone through it. Somehow it reminded me of what felt like home, and helped me to anchor as I traveled in this unknown terrain with an unknown group.

I went to Arizona thinking I was going to deserts and sunshine. By desert I mean I thought it was going to be hot and sandy. When I officially arrived in the Southwest, the drive through New Mexico was exciting and vastly different from the

Northeast where I grew up. When we reached Tucson, it took me by surprise. The desert I imagined was sandy and sand dunes... but the desert around Tucson, I found out, has the most diverse plants and animals in the world!

I received a packet in the mail months prior and had been checking, double checking, and crossing items off the list as I prepared for this 88-day expedition. I was living on beans and dented cans of food at the time, so I was trying to make what I currently owned fit the list. Since purchasing new gear was out of the question, I had to borrow most things from friends.

One of the items listed was a raincoat. Now I had in my mind that we were going to the desert, and it doesn't rain in the desert. I didn't have a raincoat, but what I did have was a thick, green plastic poncho. As we packed our bags at base, the instructors checked everything going into our bag. I clearly remember convincing the instructor that this extra thick plastic poncho with plastic snaps evenly spaced up the side, where the wind would blow through; would be suffice for this backpacking section.

We set out hiking down the trail on the first day. It was a beautiful sunny day, the air was dry and dust was kicked up by short bursts of wind. The dust added to the deep blue color of the sky and the sun shone a bright whitish yellow. There was a certain sweetness to the air, and everyone prepared for the next 88 days out in the backcountry.

In the beginning of our trek we walked together in a large group to get familiar with each other as well as to get comfortable with travel over this type of terrain. A short way in, we begin to have our first lessons reading the topographic maps. The instructor pulled out a map and unfolded it for us to see as he explained, "These are mountains here, and where the lines are closer together, that means it is much steeper, and these are cliffs right here. So right away we will recognize canyons."

We walked ahead until we came to a place where the trail stopped. Taking a few minutes to scout, we continued on. Trailblazing and pathfinding through the sharp cat's claw acacia that scattered the bottom of the canyon, the day melted away and the sunlight diminished. The light-colored rock of the canyon grew darker. At one point the canyon got so slim we were forced to learn cold water crossings. There was no choice but to swim in boots, sports bra, and shorts, pushing my backpack and swimming next to creatures I've only seen in biology class. This water was colder than the Maine ocean!

We were on an adventure of a lifetime and I was immersed in the hands-on learning experience I was looking for. Each morning I awoke to frozen boots and learned to dry my clothes with my body heat while sleeping. We walked everyday through the canyons and then up into the mountains.

As we hiked in the mountains, the air got colder the higher in elevation we went. It had been a mixture of snow and rain for days as we hiked through dense fog on the ridge. With frozen boots and cold feet, I hiked on. The poncho caught on the beautiful twisted branches of the manzanita trees and I had to tug on it a little to keep going. These trees have smooth bark, with layers of colors from reds to oranges and yellows. They are stalky like shrubs. The twisted and gnarly branches kept grabbing hold of my green plastic poncho holding it tight in it's branches. Tug and go, tug and go—this became rather monotonous. It was very hard not to take it personally. Slowly the poncho began to tear. With each snag on the trees, the plastic ripped a little more. The water began to soak my underlayers...the tear got bigger and then I found myself trapped in the small trees. Pulling myself loose, the tear split the poncho straight up the back.

The group stopped and tried to duct tape the rip, because everything is supposedly fixed with duct tape. But this tape had no interest in sticking to the soaked poncho, which was wet on both sides by now. There was no sewing kit; somehow we had all left that behind. That likely wouldn't have worked on plastic anyway.

So we now found ourselves bushwhacking through manzanita and cat's claw and at one point I pushed my way through, only to find that my poncho had been completely ripped off on my route through the trees. So I had to backtrack to retrieve the thing. By this time I was soaked, and shivering. I was cold and trying very hard to turn the corners of my mouth up using the frozen muscles of my face. I realized then, looking out around me, at the people working together, the beautiful mystical land, that it does rain and it does get cold in the desert. I should have listened to that instructor! And I realized how lucky I was to be with these amazing and caring people.

As we hiked on, we left the high ridge and headed down the eastern face of the mountains. We had made it through the rain and cold to a warmer climate. I was happy to be in my shorts after ditching the long underwear. My hand-me-down shorts hung just below my knees. They were army green with multiple pockets on each side. They fit just enough to stay on...but if I lost any weight they wouldn't have stayed up. Somewhere along the way between the poncho incident and gas stove fire under the open floor tent, I had lost the button on these shorts. And now as we hiked, I had to keep pulling them up. I tried tying them, but the rope didn't keep them tight, they only fell down as I walked and the zipper opened up. Duct tape again in this instance was a fail.

Well at least the sun came out and had dried everything, and we were headed down the mountains and out onto flatter land. We walked across beautiful terrain and most excitingly—this day was finally the day to hike without the instructors!

I preferred to walk in silence that day on my hike. I looked at the trees, held my shorts up, and enjoyed my time in the wilderness. In my search to correct the issue with my shorts, I had asked everyone for a sewing kit. No sewing kits, no needles, no buttons. I said out loud to the trees, "Please, can someone help me? All I need is a sewing kit and a button." We hiked and stopped and hiked again. Step, step, pull up shorts, step, step. It was a rather short hike and wasn't very long until we arrived at camp.

Since we were in the desert, we often camped next to the water collectors for the free-range cattle. I was first to arrive and took my empty Nalgene water bottle to the trough and dunked it in. The bottle began to fill with water. The metal container that held the water was about shoulder high, and the water was almost an arm's length below so I couldn't see it filling, I could only hear the glug and the bubbles of air escaping as the water replaced the air in the bottle.

As the bottle filled, I felt something flutter around so I pulled my Nalgene out of the trough and looked in. There was something floating in it! "What the heck?" I had caught something. I shook it around in the bottle to get a good grasp on it, and then pulled it out. It was an old plastic zip lock bag. The plastic bag was a little cloudy and hard to see inside, yet when I opened it there was a tiny sewing kit and a button inside. What are the chances? I thought. Then I said out loud, "Oh this is so perfect, thank you!" And since we were having the rest of the day off, I laid my foam pad sleeping mat in the sun, "yard-saled" all my belongings by laying everything out and hanging them so they could dry, and sewed the new button on my shorts. It was a good day. The appreciation I felt for small miracles grew tremendously that day.

We finished our backpacking section and made the transition to life on the river in a canoe. We would be living on these little crafts paddling down the Rio Grande for the next 119 miles. We traveled in pods, sometimes rafting up and floating together. We were very low in the canyon, and we could see where the water had once run 40 feet up the canyon walls. In some places our canoes dragged the bottom, and some places we actually had to get out and drag our canoes to deeper water. The water had been syphoned off for the citrus trees that were farmed in these areas. This awareness took my breath away, as it was clear how much water there used to be in this area of the river.

On this section of the trip we paddled down the river for days on end, stopping to swim, eat, and camp. We moved gracefully (most of the time) through canyons and desert. Everynight, I set my sleeping bag under the stars in the lush riparian areas by the edge of the river. Some days the afternoon winds and downpours came, and some days it was so clear and calm that we night paddled under the clear star lit sky.

We went without clocks or watches and observed the setting and rising of the sun. I lay beneath the starry night sky, watching as the big dipper circled the north star like a clock. The group had been traveling and working together so well, we were becoming synchronized. Even on the days we were silent without using watches, we were able to meet and communicate very well. It was fascinating to me to experience what happens when you reach this resonance as a group. It was an absolutely amazing experience.

We stopped at the marked location on our maps. An "X" drawn by instructors who had been through this way before, marked a hot spring and petroglyph site. The petroglyphs were rocket ships carved into the overhanging stone many years before. I was amazed! Here were these ancient carvings, way out in the wilderness with rockets and beings carved into the stone. What do these depict? What is the story? In deep thought, I soaked in the hot water trying not to get any water in my mouth or nose, highly aware of possible parasites.

After a good soak, we walked back along the thin trail and popped out on the rocky shore. Immediately something felt off, some of our canoes were moved, and some clothing scattered. Not at all "bomb proofed" as our teachers had instructed. There was a cow getting into our canoes! Wait a minute...the cow was eating someone's shirt! The boy whose shirt it was, began to chase the cow. He tried to grab the shirt that was partially hanging out while the other part was halfway down the cow's throat. Then another student tried to corner the cow and grab the shirt. All the commotion startled the cow which stumbled and bucked and stirred up all of the canoes tied at the shore before attempting to run up the canyon wall. The walls were steep and rocks came tumbling down. The cow would make some progress up, and then tumble down. I felt so bad for this animal. Some of the students were terrified and afraid of Mad Cow disease that had been in the news before we left for the trip. The cow managed to get away and the shirt was returned to its owner, wrinkled and slimy, but intact and still wearable. After a nice relaxing soak, and a minor upheaval of emotions, we were back out on the river headed to the next camp.

"Is this yours?" Someone returned a Lemurian seed quartz crystal that I left sitting on the "Groover." The groover was another name for the portable toilet that we carried with us while canoeing on the Rio to minimize our impact on the land.

I carried that Lemurian quartz crystal with me everywhere. It was a long point, maybe eight inches long, and though it wasn't that small, it was elusive. I heard through stories that these were powerful crystals with minds of their own, and somehow I believed that—and mine had the mind to keep disappearing. Some of the stories I heard about these crystals were that if you slept with one under your pillow for three nights, it would become attuned to you. So that is what I did, I kept it under my "pillow" made from my down vest when I slept at night. It made for a bumpy pillow, but it would be worth it. I was told to breathe on the crystal three times and it would be activated to me. So I did that, too, and then waited for the activation. Looking back I'm not sure what having a crystal attuned or activated to me would do, but it sounded neat.

We arrived at the next camp at near dark; we had been paddling all day long and were eager to get set up and begin dinner. The breeze blew cool air as the night began to settle in and we made hot drinks and dinner over the WhisperLite stoves. I felt my pocket. I had been so busy I didn't notice but that crystal was gone! I crawled into my sleeping bag, arms tired and weary from the day. "I'll find it tomorrow," I convinced myself. The next morning I woke up and rolled over. I got up with the sun and looked all over, but that magical crystal had disappeared.

"Those crystals really do have a mind of their own," I thought, a little disappointed in it's disappearance. Perhaps it had gone to another dimension or to help someone else.

Night paddling under the clear starlit sky the last early morning of the canoe section was one of the most incredible experiences I have ever had. The air was calm, the purples and dark blues behind the stars illuminated their presence. The reflection from the moon swirled as each paddle was dipped into the water, leaving tiny swirls and eddies behind each canoe. The smell of the damp earth and the riparian edge filled my senses. This was a silent excitement, those moments where butterflies dance in your gut, bubbling over yet each person has vowed silence in paddling together toward the ending of one section and toward the beginning of something new. We couldn't exactly see where we were going physically and that was in itself amazing. What a moment—to be on the water as the sun rose gently warming the earth, giving color and texture to the river banks and accenting the plants that held the edge in its place. To see the water and its reflections change in the morning light, and to witness the light as the day begins.

Another section was closing, and a new one would be opening. We switched gears by unpacking, cleaning, and repacking. This time we were back at the Tucson NOLS base and they set us up with showers at the local YMCA. After the showers they brought us to thrift shops to search for clothes suitable for caving. Onesies, or one piece suits were suggested, the instructors had a minimalist approach. They explained this was to minimize the possibility of leaving anything behind in the caves. We didn't even want to leave threads or fuzz from our clothes. There would be times where we would be crawling and squeezing through small spaces, and the less buttons and snags the better. Everyone searched through the used clothes since we knew they would get very dirty anyway.

While looking through a rack of clothes, a friend suggested the bookstore across the street. So while everyone else continued shopping, we crossed the busy street and made our way to the bookstore.

When I entered through the doors, I saw shelves upon shelves of used books. I wandered the aisles browsing and scanning the many bindings until one popped out to me, The Starseed Transmissions. "Well that sounds interesting," I thought. When I pulled the book from the shelf, another green book fell to the floor with a loud thud. I looked around, embarrassed to be disturbing the quiet. To me it felt like it echoed through the store, but no one seemed to notice.

My heart was pounding as I bent down to pick the book from the floor and read the cover, The Celestine Prophecy. I read the inside flap of the hard cover. "Wow, sounds adventurous!" I thought as I flipped through the pages. This book had been recommended to me for years but I hadn't had any interest in it. Some of my friends even said that it changed their life. "How could a book really change someone's life?" I mumbled out loud. Maybe I was about to find out. I purchased the books and carried them with me, hoping to have time to read while at Cave Camp.

My first exposure to caving was during my semester with NOLS as a student. We camped for 16 days in the New Mexico high desert. Looking across the rolling land with sparse dry plants scattered and the wind continually blowing dust, you would never know the beauty of the caverns below. Using topographic maps and directions from other cavers, we would hike across the desert looking for a hole in the ground. Some entrances to the caves just appeared to be a hole measuring about shoulder width apart, while some caves I could walk right in, and others I had to hold my breath, squeeze through a small space, and crawl just to get around. The area where we set up Cave Camp was all limestone. This was a giant coral reef at one time. Limestone dissolves very easily with water and that is how the many caves and cave systems in that specific area in New Mexico were created over thousands of years.

One cave we visited in particular, really stands out in my memory. Walking uphill a little way there was a small hidden entrance to the cave. It couldn't be seen from the trail below. Looking down into the opening, all we could see was darkness. I tried to focus my eyes and still nothing; no depth, no bottom, no light. Nothing. This only made me more curious. We set up an above ground anchor outside of the entrance which was a small hole about shoulder width apart. Then the instructor went in feet first, and rappelled down into the cave on the fixed rope held securely by the anchor we had just built.

The thought of going backwards through a hole in the ground, not knowing what might be in there, was a little frightening. I tightened the straps around my thighs and double checked the buckles on the harness around my waist. I yelled down, and shook the rope to alert the instructor that I would begin my descent into the cave. I heard the instructor yell back and felt the tug on the rope. At the bottom of the rope, the instructor held it loosely as a backup safety measure so I wouldn't fall. I couldn't see her, but I knew by the tug on the rope that she was there and ready. I began my descent through the top layer of the earth. The rope was fixed to the anchor and fed through a friction device that was attached to my harness. This was so I could move slowly. The more friction, the slower I would go.

Once inside the cave, I realized I was just hanging on a rope. There was no earth to stand on and nothing to hold on to. The air was very still, and the earthy smell filled my nose. It literally was a different world under the surface. My helmet had a head lamp attached so I could see what was around me. I spun myself around to take a look. This underground room was very large. The depth from the entrance to the bottom was about 200 feet! What I saw was the most amazing thing that I could ever imagine. There were stalactites that looked like melting wax coming from the ceiling, and stalagmites growing up from the ground in the shape of a giant mushroom castle. There were ribbons of stone like draperies hung from the ceiling. It was spectacular. I locked myself on the rope with my friction device so I wouldn't move and clicked off my head lamp. There I hung, in complete darkness. It was so dark I couldn't see my hands in front of me. Yes I tried to, I took my hands off the rope and moved them around. I was securely locked by friction and waving my arms around about 100 feet off the floor. Then I settled in and enjoyed the moment. The deep stillness I felt was like no other feeling I had experienced before. It almost made me lose track of my thoughts and time. There was no outer reference for space, no light, and no indicators of the passing of time besides my own breath and heartbeat. Never would I have another moment just like that. I turned my head lamp back on and continued my descent. Once landing softly on the floor, I disconnected from the rope and looked around. This place was immense, I was in complete awe, that is the only way I could describe it. We explored a variety of caves in the area until the end of the caving section.

Then we hit the road to Cochise Stronghold in Arizona for the next section of my NOLS semester. We parked the cars, unloaded, and ventured down the path toward our next episode of the adventure. After walking 10 miles through the ancient granite by foot, we finally arrived at "Climb Camp," which would serve as our base camp for the next section. Looking around, we chose our group camps and imagined our kitchen setups before finally settling in. This turned out to be a very good rest day to help us transition from being on the river, to being on the rock.

We went through all the regular climbing classes: gear, rope handling, harnesses, belaying, and communication. Looking back, this course was a lot different than what I first imagined.

I woke early before the sun to boil water for tea which I carried to the morning circle with my foam pad and journal. Each morning began with yoga, a gentle moving and awakening of my body with the rising sun. I would peel off my layers of clothing as the day warmed and so with it, my body. Gentle movements and stretches were followed by quiet meditation. At first I didn't see what yoga and meditation had to do with climbing. It was interesting and fun, sure, but I was so eager to climb. As the days went on and I continued the practice, I was able to bring the breathing and mindfulness to calm my mind while moving on the rock. It helped me to pay attention to the thoughts in my head, and to realize what I was thinking before I accomplished a sweet challenging move or the thoughts I had before a fall.

During the climbing section they offered a short solo experience where we could go off on our own for a few days. At that time in my life I didn't exactly want to go sit by myself. The fear present at that moment, as I recognize it now, was being afraid to be alone with my thoughts. I was unsure if I could just 'be with me' for even 24 hours. But I wanted to try anyway, knowing that I could always go back to camp. I brought a bagel and two Nalgenes of water with me. My feet wandered over the rocks and between the old granite boulders trying to feel out a good place to rest for the next full day. I imagined a spot with a really good view, and I also wanted a nice private, secure place tucked into the rocks. After climbing up and down I finally settled on a nice flat rock and set myself up looking to the west. I tried meditating like our instructor had shown us, but quickly got discouraged as my mind jumped around to many topics. I debated taking off all my clothes. There might have been voices in the distance; I thought I had heard people talking but wasn't sure. I was afraid someone would stumble upon me, in my private solo space. I imagined that would be awkward!

Our instructors had suggested writing a letter to ourselves for the future and so I brought one piece of paper and a pencil with me. It took all day and part of the night, but I was finally able to settle in. The panoramic view of the sunset was immensely beautiful. The soft, pink glow as the sun dipped below the horizon, shone on the exposed rock and the spiky leaves of the yucca. The changing light accentuated the textures and details around me as far as I could see. The sound of the whippoorwill came from a small grove of trees nearby. The cooper's hawks flew overhead. I even saw the cumbersome tarantula walk in a slow zig zag across the land. I managed to find peace in that moment. With the disappearing light, I took a deep breath, wrote a letter to my future self, and calmly drifted off to sleep.

I awoke the next morning to a big bumble bee checking on me. I sat up and the bee was right in my face. "What are you doing here?" I whispered in a crackly voice. "Have I gone mad now talking with the insects?" I thought to myself.

Maybe I had run out of things to do. I always had something in my hands to work on. I was usually beading or embroidering while traveling, or sewing quilts and clothes while I was home. I loved to craft. I didn't have anything with me on this solo section, so I began to hollow out a yucca stalk in the hopes of making a small didgeridoo. The inside was soft, and the outer shell was hard and a little brittle. I worked intently on this carving until our solo time was up, and at that point I had gotten so comfortable with myself that I could have stayed out there longer! But I knew I wanted to climb as much as I could so my crafting fingers went from carving yucca to pinching and jamming cracks in the rock wall.

I climbed as much as I could to absorb every ounce of practice and learning. I climbed "easy" routes to feel the dance of the movements. I pushed myself to do the hardest finger cracks available, and practiced gear placement and anchor building to strengthen my technical skills. An amazing world opened up for me while I navigated the old granite at Cochise Stronghold in the Arizona sun. My comfort with myself grew, and so did my confidence.

Camped again at the NOLS base for another day, we packed and prepared for the next and final section. This time would be 10 days backpacking over 100 miles. This was the final student-led expedition. We would enter the Gila Wilderness in New Mexico and backpack together as a group for a few short days. Then we would break into small groups to navigate the Wilderness using the skills we had learned. The plan was to meet again at the "X" for the completion of the course. We had been preparing for this moment for the last 78 days when we would finally use our newly refined skills by applying them where fit, and rely on each member of the group.

I tucked the books in my pack excited for the adventure ahead and hopeful to have time to continue reading. I felt confident at this point with my map reading and cooking skills. We had planned to check out archaeological sites along the way. As we hiked, the dry high desert got to us. On the map there were lakes and small ponds, but in the real landscape those were dry, cracked mud. We hiked up high for quite some time. Living on Jolly Ranchers and cheesecake mix, we made our way across the beautiful mesas dotted with tall pines and juniper trees. We had let the boys do the rations and we ended up with way too much food. They had rationed mostly cheesecake mix and Jolly Ranchers. What were we thinking to not double check? I had just packed everything without even looking

I had begun to read The Starseed Transmissions and found it an interesting read. Each night at camp I would settle in my sleeping bag, turn on my headlamp, write in my journal and then flip through the pages enthralled by the story. I wanted to enjoy every moment, to capture this adventure, and to savor this experience out here in the desert of New Mexico.

One night after I had put my books down and had fallen asleep, I heard a rustle nearby. I thought my tent mates were still awake and making noise. I opened my eyes and looked into the darkness. It looked like they had their headlamps on and were running up and down the hill nearby. What the heck were they doing? I rolled over and went back to sleep. When I woke in the morning and looked in that direction, there was no hill, and no bushes. I asked my group mates what they had been doing, but they said they hadn't gotten up. So what had I seen? It was a curious incident, one that has never left my mind.

We carried on hiking in silence with our heavy packs, dehydrated from the combination of dry cheesecake mix and no water. We hiked over high desert and dry terrain for over 10 miles. This felt like forever walking in the unknown with every image of the skeleton beneath the cactus that I had seen on the T-shirts and magnets in the gift shop. Would I end up like that?

Finally we reached a brown puddle of muddy water below a small hill. I prepared my Aquamira water treatment. And then I took a seat and waited for water treatment to turn bright yellow, the indicator that it was ready to be added to the murky water. I happened to look up toward the top of the hill. At the top of the hill I could see something I didn't recognize, like an animal laying on its side. My stomach turned as I realized there was a carcass of a large animal lying at the top of the hill. I imagined that this water that I was about to collect to quench my thirst must have come down over that dead carcass and into the puddle below. I felt nauseous and immediately poured the water onto the ground. I just couldn't do it. So instead we kept on hiking.

We hiked another 10 miles across the hot and dusty desert in search of cool refreshing water. On the map there were lakes and creeks pictured every few miles. But in reality the area was in a deep drought. The "creeks" were sandy beds that once flowed, or dried cracked mud where the lakes used to be. We entered a small canyon and could feel a shift in the air. It felt cool and damp. As we followed the canyon, the rock walls grew taller on both sides. We found ourselves stumbling over branches, rocks and boulders wedged in the bottom of the slot canyon. The air was musty and damp and felt cool on my skin.

I turned a corner and was filled with hope as I saw the rock wall ahead of me covered with bright green with moss. Moving directly in the direction of the mossy wall, I saw water dripping from the ends of the tiny plants. Placing my Nalgene water bottle under the dripping water, I held it there collecting each fresh drip one by one. When there was enough to drink, I drank it up and began to fill it again. It was slow of course, but the cool water was so refreshing after traveling so many dusty, thirsty miles.

The water absorbed into my skin and soothed my dry, cracked lips. All the cells in my body began to absorb the water and I felt a rush of energy and aliveness come back to my being. The importance of water was brought to my full attention during those miles, an awareness I wouldn't have had otherwise.

After hours in that spot quenching my thirst, we decided to move down the canyon. When we came out at the mouth of the canyon, we connected with the West Branch of the Gila River. That water was flowing, clear, and cool. It felt like arriving in paradise. We waited so long, and this was just around the corner! We threw our packs down on the gravel, took our shoes off, and laid down in the cool water. Later we got our foam sleeping pads out and tried "rafting" down the stream. We played the whole afternoon singing and splashing around in the cool, refreshing water. We set camp there for the evening, drifting off to sleep with the sound of the water tumbling over the rocks. Our thirst quenched and feeling revitalized, we were ready for the next leg of the trip.

7. Committed to the Path

I n college my concentration in Outdoor Education was Adventure Education and Wilderness Leadership. It was pretty awesome to have classes in backpacking, rock climbing, whitewater rafting, canoeing, and ropes course challenges, because we had to participate in these activities to learn about them—score!

At that time I would describe myself as fit and very active. My dreams were big and I went out of my way to make those dreams a reality with determination. No matter if my knees were shaking or my voice wavered when I spoke, I moved forward, chasing those fantastic dreams. No matter what, I was determined to move closer to those realities.

I made phone calls when I was afraid to, applied for things that I thought were too big of a stretch, and talked to people about what it was that I wanted to accomplish. This led me to amazing experiences and opportunities for growth that in turn strengthened my character and built who I have become today. Those experiences pulled more from me, from my inner space, than I ever thought or knew existed.

During my final year of college, I worked as hard as I could imagine. I needed 22 credits per semester to graduate that year and I wasn't going to settle for anything less. I wanted to be a Wilderness Guide (which I re-established on my eighty-eight day semester in the Southwest.)

The real life wilderness experience had changed me drastically. Adventuring in new landscapes with new people for extended periods sparked within me a greater awareness of who I was and who I could become. The change was huge for me, not so much from the outside, but from the inside. I grew confidence in my leadership and wilderness skills that I didn't know was there before.

During my last year of college I "worked" very long days. I needed to complete and document my credits as well as the leadership days that were required for my major. My goal each day was to find every opportunity to practice, gain experience, have fun, and learn. I began planning outings for the outing club and volunteering for the Vermont Special Olympics. I guided snowshoe tours in the woods at Ben and Jerry's Ice Cream Factory. I scoured bulletin boards and local papers, and talked with those around me to find out what was out there. The potential was endless.

What I didn't share was that what I saw around me was a world hurting, where people were afraid to be themselves, and afraid to be real. I wanted to do my best to make a change in this world, or at least in my own life.

I had committed and wanted to see that commitment through often working many 15-hour days in a row. "What can I do as a human in this world, to help others to be more real, and to be happier?" There is more to life than this!

I invited elementary school kids to visit the college. I organized volunteers to help lead large group games in the gym. I began a reading program at the public library that was focused on building community. I put everything I had into everything I did, and yet, it still did not seem to be enough. When the day was over, I would curl up on my twin-sized mattress in the corner of the room on the floor. With a sigh of relief I'd relax with a book and get lost in my imagination for hours. Sometimes it was hard to stay focused on my book while music blared from the room below me. My roommates were still into partying then, but I had seen a glimmer of something else, something beyond.

I remember being in my bedroom one day. The door jostled as they banged on the old wooden door begging me to come join the party. They couldn't understand why I didn't want to leave my room. But, I was exactly where I wanted to be—dreaming up an incredible life.

I remember going across the street to the payphone with a calling card that my mom had sent in the mail. Pressing each sticky button to dial the number of an old friend. "I am going to change the world," I said, full of hope. "I will find a way." I assured the person on the other end of the line, but actually hearing it out loud was reassuring myself.

"For now I am helping young kids to read. I have started a very successful reading group for preschoolers to help bring the community together. The kids are reading and exploring the books through fun activities." I knew I wanted to have an impact in the world, and that was my plan at the time. I saw the importance of community, especially with moms and their kids finding fun, empowerment through education and support.

In my little spare time, I indulged in reading Way of the Peaceful Warrior. I remember saying, "I want my life to be like that. I want to meet a master, a teacher." I asked the universe to send me a teacher, yet I wasn't clear in my mind what that actually looked like.

As I began to pay more attention to my life and surroundings, I put my focus on reading, dreaming, journaling, community, and being of service. This shift created an avenue for so many opportunities to come my way. I had dreamed of a nice home, with space to read, journal, imagine, and play in the woods. It wasn't always present where I lived. Mumbling out loud as I went about my day, I would say all of the things I dreamed and wanted, careful not to let anyone hear me talking to myself!

And one rainy Monday, I came into the library to get ready for the reading program. I was putting the crayons and markers out and rolling out the big paper when the librarian approached me. She explained that she would be traveling for a little while and wondered if I could watch their house while they were gone. Of course I would!

So I went over after the reading program to take a look. I would be taking care of the dog and feeding the fish. In return, I had my own bedroom with a cozy futon, and she would pay me! Plus I could eat anything in the house, and she gave me extra money for groceries. A college student's dream!

This was even more than I had imagined. At the front of the home was a giant picture window with a clear view of the tall Vermont mountains. The house was set on a hill. The land and the area was quiet, gorgeous, and expansive, I felt like I was on retreat just being there.

The day I came over to pick up the key, she went over everything I would need to know. I met the long-haired, friendly and playful dog, and learned where everything was. She had written all of the instructions and information on a notepad in case I needed it and said she would check in every so often.

The day came when the librarian and her family departed for their trip and I stopped by soon after my classes were over for the day. I put the key in the doorknob, turned it slightly and the door popped open no problem. The dog was very happy to see me as I carefully entered the house. After our greeting, I let her out the door and we both played outside for a while.

Soon it began to get cold and I was ready to go back inside. I put my hand on the knob and tried to open the door, but the knob didn't turn. The door was locked. "Oh no." I started to panic. How could living my dream and feeling so free and amazing suddenly disappear in a matter of touching a door knob? My heart and mind raced. From calm and freedom to panic!

I came to the realization that I had locked myself out and the key was sitting on the table. At the same time, I also realized that the cordless phone was inside the house sitting on the notepad. Scurrying around the house, I checked every window hoping one would be unlocked. But they were all locked! What was I going to do? The dog was looking at me ready to go inside, yet I couldn't figure out how. I got in my white Toyota Tercel and tried to focus. Breathing calmed me so I could think more clearly. Looking at the house I said out loud, "What can I do?"

Then I patiently waited for an answer with my eyes open. A window that I hadn't tried yet stood out to me. It was higher than the others so I couldn't see inside from ground level and had skipped over it. The small shed looked promising in my search for something to stand on. The step ladder was easy to grab and I quickly dragged it over to the window. I looked around to make sure no one was watching. I would be able to explain myself if someone happened to see me breaking in, but out in the middle of the woods luckily I saw no one. Not a soul. No one to help and no one to accuse me of breaking in. So I climbed up the ladder.

Peeking through the glass, I was relieved to see the latch was unlocked. I took the screen off and leaned it up against the house. Then placed my palms on the outside of the glass and carefully pushed up. The window slid up to reveal a collection of tiny trinkets and glass objects lining the window sill. This fragile collection was right above the kitchen sink. The big metal kitchen sink. I climbed up as high as I could on the step ladder, wobbling on the very top with my feet on the sticker that warns not to stand there. Then carefully I stepped one foot through the window, avoiding any of the breakable keepsakes. I steadied myself with one foot in the sink, and one on the ladder out the window. I moved each trinket one by one so they wouldn't topple into the sink. "Steady now," I kept telling myself as my whole body was shaking out of nervousness, adrenaline, and muscle fatigue from holding this awkward position.

It sure would look like I was breaking into this house if anyone arrived! My senses were on high alert. My hearing sharpened, my mind raced, my heart beat heavily in my chest, and my breath quickened. I just wanted to get this over with—to be in the house and able to let the dog in. The dog was watching my every move so intently. Shaking uncontrollably, I managed to squeeze my body through the window and found myself standing in the sink. I was inside. I paused for a breath of relief!

Then slowly I closed the window behind me, climbed out of the sink, circled around the counter and let the dog in. I grabbed the key, put it in my pocket and returned all evidence by setting each of the tiny trinkets back in place. This was just the first half hour of my dog sitting gig, I hoped the rest would go well. I didn't want to admit that I had done this, but I called the librarian anyway. I told her about the incident, mostly in case anyone saw or thought I was breaking in. It was good to hear the librarian's voice on the other end of the phone. Once I shared what happened, she thanked me for sharing and told me not to worry about. Her son had done that many times.

More and more opportunities came to me and I had so many amazing experiences that year! The end of the year came so quickly. We had planned a trip with our class out West. We were excited to travel and to plan the whole trip. I was so excited to be going back out West again, I loved the weather, the sun, and the warmth. I had become comfortable with the plants and the animals and just how vast the landscape was. The night skies glittered with amazing stars in the deep desert sky that you just couldn't see in the East.

A friend of mine suggested we drive and take our time. We could explore and visit places along the way and then meet our class at the airport in Albuquerque, New Mexico where the group planned to fly in. And so the plan was set into motion.

My last day of college came rather quickly, I had been inside typing up my final reports all day. Maybe for three days now that I think about it. What a relief to be complete with most of my work! I walked outside from the computer building and across the parking lot to my little Toyota that was parked at a slight angle. I got in my car and went to play the CD that was in the player. For some reason, the stereo was pulled out a little ways. I thought this was strange. I popped in the album The

Arista Years and began singing along one of my favorite songs that got me through hard places in my life. I belted out "Built To Last" like no one was listening, because they weren't.

As I was singing, I looked around. Something felt off. I was halfway down the hill from school when I realized everything in my car was gone! I drove to the grocery store and got out of my car. Shaking I dropped the quarters in the payphone and dialed. My mom answered and I explained. "Everything is gone. My beaded seat cover, the vanilla tree air freshener, and even a bag packed with somewhat clean clothes. My favorite 1980's purple wind suit that Dad gave me with the green stripes down the outer legs, my camp stove, my clothes, most everything is gone." My mom, in her calm voice, told me to slow down and explain what happened. Luckily my sleeping bag was locked in the trunk, but that was it. I had been packing for a five-day Leave No Trace Master Educator backpacking course in the White Mountains that was starting in just a few days. The course was part of my requirements to graduate college.

Although I was frantic, everyone around me helped out so much. From borrowing a red backpack from my college and shopping at L.L.Bean with my mom, to borrowing from friends, I was able to prepare for the five-day trip.

Right after the completion of that course, my friend would pick me up and we would head cross country for a three-month adventure that would include the white water rafting and back-packing with our Wilderness Leadership Techniques class out in New Mexico. I felt prepared enough to make the trek.

I had been practicing driving the van around Burlington to get used to the 1993 Eurovan. At first I had a hard time, then we realized the clutch was going and needed to be replaced. So this time driving across the country listening to the mini disc in the 1993 teal-colored Eurovan, we took it slow on the highway. We stopped at the rest areas to sleep and made our way toward Colorado.

The land was pretty flat and easy going. Peering out the windows at the windmills and rolling hills, Ohio seemed boring, yet we knew it would be days before we would get to see the Rockies and kept that image in our minds.

My friend slept in the back as we cruised down the highway. I felt happy and carefree, grateful for this experience and the adventure ahead. And then something strange happened. Driving along the gear shifter popped out of fifth into neutral. "Huh that's weird. Hey, your van just popped out of fifth, what should I do?" I asked my friend. I put it back in gear and we drove some more. He said, "We will get off at the next exit." But before we made it to the exit, the shifter popped out and it made an intense grinding and rattling sound that made us cringe. It just didn't sound good at all.

We switched spots and he drove as I winced and covered my ears. The only gear the van would go into was third. It sounded bad. It sounded really bad. We got to a gas station off the exit, chugging and bucking uphill finally coming to a stop. Everyone who came by to see what was happening said the same thing, "It doesn't sound good."

So there we were in Nebraska, with a blown transmission. We had the car towed to a Volkswagen dealer, who couldn't help us, so it towed the car to a transmission expert. He said he could fix it, so we waited for several days while he took it all apart. Once he got that far he realized that transmission was beyond repair. And we were stuck in Omaha, Nebraska for four very long days. My longing for the Colorado mountains grew stronger as I peered out of the hotel window at the sprawling city all around me.

Looking around the hotel gift shop I flipped through the t-shirts. I got to one maroon one with a picture of a wagon wheel, and it read, "Nebraska, we got nothin'!" Oh my I laughed so hard, I bought that shirt and put it right on.

Omaha apparently was known for their zoo, that's what the desk clerk told me anyway. She also told me they had a new bead store nearby. The shuttle from the hotel brought me there and dropped me off. I browsed through the thousands of beads! After I spent about $200 I called the shuttle for pickup. I went back to the hotel and began to bead. I made several bead woven bracelets and had ideas for necklaces. These I could sell along the way to help with gas, meals, and repairs.

In the meantime we asked what else people do around there. "Well some go to the Poop Deck." "What? The Poop Deck? What the heck is that?" It was a local dive right up the street. So we walked there, it wasn't too far. We went in. There were a few guys sitting at the bar. I ordered a Jameson and ginger ale. "Excuse me? A what? You are in the Midwest, we don't have ginger ale, but we can make it." "Ok sure that sounds good. What do you make ginger ale out of?"

They had a digital scoring (and talking) dart machine there so we began to play. The bartender then gave me a few drinks on the house. He said, "You can't walk into my bar at two in the afternoon, order a Jameson and ginger, and walk out of here." I thought that was an interesting comment but I accepted the drink anyway.

Soon I realized it was just too much alcohol in one drink, however we continued the darts. Somehow by evening I managed to trade the bartender and owner the black hat I was wearing for a Jack Daniels trucker hat. Later when we got back to the hotel, I realized this hat was the bartender's and I got nauseous thinking about his sweaty head in that hat. I dunked the hat in the sink and scrubbed it with the small bottles of shampoo, scrubbing and scrubbing. If this hat was going to be mine, it was going to be clean.

When the van was fixed, we hit the road again and headed as far from Omaha as possible. Now I had a bunch of beads, needles, and thread, so beading became my pastime when I wasn't driving. I started an inventory of one-of-a-kind bead woven bracelets that were inspired by the land, rivers, and mountains around me.

We traveled easily across the flat country that slowly turned to rolling hills. Finally when those mountains peeked above the horizon and rose slowly in front of us, I kept my focus forward. Then came the golden moment, yet this teal van could barely make it up the hill. I was nervous, with cars and trucks squealing by us as we puttered our way up the hill toward the next adventure. "I think I can, I think I can, I really hope we can...."

We met up with two college classmates at their campsite in Leadville, Colorado. Leadville claims to be the highest established town. The town was up there at 10,152 feet above sea level. It took some time to get used to, the air was thin and because of the lesser amount of oxygen, my muscles were fatigued.

Despite the slow movement, we managed a slow game of disc golf with lots of rests before heading back down the mountains and toward the desert. We traveled and camped as we made our way down to Albuquerque, New Mexico. We rolled up to pick up our classmates who had flown out West for our Wilderness Leadership Techniques class. I pull up in the teal van, wearing the Jack Daniels trucker hat and a huge smile. We had been on the road and camping for a few weeks now, and were so excited to join everyone for the next big adventure.

Everyone piled into the Eurovan and we began the tour of Farmington, New Mexico. We would base from there with the help from the local college and friends. Our first section of the trip was backpacking for eight days in the Manti-La Sal National Forest.

8. Pizza Pinwheels and the Backcountry

W e began our journey in the expansive land of red colored canyons and rugged mountains in Utah. This terrain was much different than that of the Northeast that we were used to. Each day we elected a new "Leader of the Day" to practice planning and executing backcountry travel.

The students in my college class were charged with planning the entire wilderness expedition through the National Forest in southern Utah. This would help prepare us for future jobs or leading our own expeditions in the backcountry. We decided on backpacking in the Manti-Lasal National Forest followed by a section of white water raft guide training in the Four Corners area. Psyched to be going back to the Southwest, I offered whatever I could to help make this trip a success. I felt confident in my travel skills in this environment. I felt good and prepared for the trip, and shared information only when the others asked in an attempt to not be a "NOLS it all" as my instructors had jokingly warned. "People won't take to that too well."

I shared with my group how when on my NOLS trip one person cooked while the others would take the evening off to journal or to do what they needed to. My group consisted of two women from the class and our professor. We all agreed to this idea of rotating responsibilities and taking breaks.

So after backpacking a few nights, it was my turn to cook dinner and I wanted to share with my group the best pizza pinwheels ever! I had made these before, many times actually, on a WhisperLite stove in the backcountry in the desert. I was in my element. I was pumped to be able to share what I "knew" in regards to the backpacker's kitchen. And so we had a lesson on leadership and decision-making under the trees in the central area of our temporary village, and then I left the group to prepare dinner.

Our kitchen area was set up a short distance from our meeting space nestled under the juniper trees. I got to work. Taking the food out of the duffle bags, I spread it out so I could see everything. "What can I work with?" We had flour, water, salt, pepperoni, and cheese. I was going to make the best dinner ever and for dessert I had my heart set on sharing the best cinnamon buns ever!

My tent mate had come with a fancy cook set, one that was non-stick Teflon. Never had I encountered such a luxury on my backcountry travels, but here it was! I was close enough to the group that I could hear them, but they couldn't see me. After a while they began to check in on me. "Is it ready yet?" Everyone else had already eaten, cleaned up and were playing. But I was fumbling around and yelled back, "Yup everything's good, just a minute. They're almost done." "What is taking so long?" For some reason this whole process took me forever. The non-stick pans were sticking. The grease from the cheese caused little bursts of fire as smoke rose from the stove. More cheese melted, flamed, and burnt to the pan. I spilled the flour and it puffed up in a cloud, covering me from head to toe. I was sweating, uncomfortable and dusty. So I emerged from the kitchen with the intent of letting my tent mates know that it was almost ready.

When I stood up, I felt a little resistance and heard a tearing sound. And then I felt a cool breeze… "Oh no!" My only shorts had split wide open. The rip went up the back of one leg all the way up to my waist.

On this trip I had wanted to be smart, and not carry so much gear. I would have a light pack and travel comfortably. I went so super light, in fact, I wore no underwear, and the rip went the entire length of my backside. The shorts were wide open in the back. Maybe no one would notice. Looking through my backpack I found that I didn't bring any underwear at all, or even long underwear. What was I thinking? Maybe I had packed a little too light.

So I placed the pizza pinwheels on the lid of the pan and walked over to the group holding my "masterpiece" up with both hands. The other groups had long since finished dinner and I said to my two tent mates and our professor, "Dinner is served." Then I cautiously turned around, still holding the lid and pizza pinwheels in front of me, and walked back toward the kitchen. I heard a gasp, then another. Then the whole group burst out laughing! "Full Moon!" My bare cheeks were open to the elements and to the group's eyes.

So I walked back to the kitchen and waited for my tent mates to arrive. We sat together crunching on burnt pizza pinwheels while figuring out a way to repair my shorts. Again we had no sewing kit! You would think that I would learn by now. And the duct tape wouldn't sustain a tear of this size. One of my tent mates offered a pair of bright red shorts. She was about half my size so when I pulled these shorts up they were super short, and comparable to underwear. I wore those underneath my old ripped shorts for the remainder of the trip.

Brad, our professor, offered to clean the pans. Oh boy that was a mess. The non-stick pans didn't exactly turn out to be non-stick for my infamous pizza rolls! And so much for knowing it all, my ego was smashed all over the desert that day. The cinnamon buns, however, turned out to be a substantial win in this case.

Again and again traveling the wilderness while living so close with a group gave me real, in-your-face lessons. I learned more about myself each day on that journey. Many situations arose, and how we worked through those together was amazing. I found myself opening up from that shy and introverted place to feel more compassion for myself and the members of the group. We all had our moments of learning; it happens out there in the wilderness. You can't run, you can't hide. You have to face every bit of yourself and your emotions.

With each step on the trail, I was able to carve away untruths. By experiencing real moments of connection and communication I saw more beauty in my life and in the landscape around me. I saw how powerfully the wilderness pulled us together. This kept me laughing and feeling alive! There is so much to life, and so much more we can experience together.

Each day we focused on where we were going. I mean, it felt like that's all we looked at, the end result. The slushies or margaritas at the end of the trip. The direction was to get to the next spot and follow the time control plan that we had established. I wasn't much into planning time, and lived a free spirit. But I was out there to learn how to take others into the wild to experience these things, and so I did my best.

We were as a group, though, always looking to do the next thing. One morning as I woke I thought, "I am going to want to remember this moment, this trip." There will never be anything like this again, or with these people, with these lessons. And with the sun blaring, loudly announcing its presence upon sunrise, I wrote a reflection of the trip. The ups and downs, the learning, the small moments with each other that held so much meaning. Those reasons that brought me to the wilderness again and again, and those moments shared with others that held special meaning. Eventually I read that reflection poem to the group. It's important to enjoy the moments as they are always changing. Can you capture the feeling of an interaction with the sunset? Can you hold an incredible moment with your words?

These moments feel more real than the everyday mundane that we walk through in 'regular' life. The patterns, the jobs, the red lights and green lights, the grocery stores...out here in The Wild, things are different. Time slows and you have the opportunity to expand. To live in the present. To change course, to stop and enjoy a moment. There is a realness that emerges, because it has to. You can't hide, you are with the same people so conflicts must be confronted. Your clothing has to be functional, not just look good. The plan becomes to stay warm, dry, fed, and happy. Everything else falls away.

I knew that I wanted to bring others into the wilderness. To find themselves. To find what is real for them. When you slow down and listen to the earth, you begin to hear yourself. At first your breath, and then your struggles, and then your deepest passions and what drives you to be alive and to keep going each day. And so I committed to this as my work. To guide others into the wilderness, full knowing that it would guide them on an exploration of self.

For the next section we switched gears for our white water rafting class. We chased the water before it flowed out for the summer, each morning checking the rivers and flow. Snow melt makes the rivers swell, but the rush only lasts a short while. It was so good to see the world from this new perspective. To see the edges of the river by floating in it, to see the canyon walls pass by above us. To feel the rush as we go full force into a standing wave, and drink the splashes as we hit the next train of waves. The river is a different environment, and forces open different fears as well as new skills to be learned. We had to learn to communicate and work together in a whole new way, with safety as a priority. We had lots of fun and many Dutch oven meals before the class was over. Soon we were back in the van again heading north once more.

We were on our way to pick up my friend who had traveled an arduous long trip across the country to come meet us. We planned to travel together for several months, to climb, and to catch some outdoor concerts. I have to say looking back and writing I'm a little disappointed as my dreams were much higher than we actually made time for. We did travel and camp and got a good system down. We had a cooler, stopped at the grocery store, and had sandwiches on the road. I found my favorite pair of flip flops in a grocery store in San Diego and I was so happy. I'd been wearing hot and heavy day hikers all through Arizona. What a relief.

Our travels took us down many roads, and not much climbing. We went mining crystals, ended up at a rainbow gathering, and visited the giant trees in the Pacific Northwest. We had fires on the beaches and slept under the stars traveling all the way up the coast to Seattle. We flew back to Burlington, Vermont and somehow I managed to make it back to Maine and my hometown. It had been a long journey.

I was ready to get a little more serious with my work and my life, and my deep desire to help others grew strong. It felt strange to not have to go back to Johnson, Vermont. I had finished my course work and all that was left was my internship. I searched for one that would be close by and fun, as well as providing me lots of field experience.

9. Finding My Teacher

My grandfather, Romeo, would work a little and then say out of the blue, "Smoke 'em if you got 'em," as he walked toward the shade by the trees. He was born in Canada with French as his first language, and had lived in Maine most of his life so he had a unique accent sometimes combining French and English words or making up his own. We just started working, and now we are going to stop and sit in the shade? Neither of us smoked, we just sat and rested. He just used that saying from working with crews all his life.

When he saw my frustration with how many times we stopped, he told me, "You have to work smart, not hard." This has to be my favorite teaching from my grandfather. So we worked at a good pace all day, preserving our energy. We did a variety of work—I never knew what he would have for me that day when I showed up. We cut brush, patched the roof, and hosed off carpet squares on the tarred driveway. He even had me repairing the hole in the garage and jacking up the barn. That is a story for another time!

With a sly smile, my grandfather asked me to go on a walk with him one morning. So we took our time strolling around the block. As we turned the corner, I could see there was an older house having some renovations done. My grandfather smiled and pointed to the dumpster outside the house on the lawn. "Watch out for the nails," he said as he made a motion with his hand, telling me to climb in. Apprehensively, I walked over to the dumpster and did as he asked, dropping down on a pile of boards. I rummaged through the pile looking for wide barn boards, they don't make them like that anymore, and that is what he wanted. I found a few, so we walked back home and grabbed the trailer.

Next thing, I was back in the dumpster pulling out good, wide boards. I felt like I was stealing these and was hoping that no one I knew would go by in the midst of this endeavor. I wouldn't want to admit to anyone that I was dumpster-diving, even if it was on my grandfather's behalf. When we had a good pile of boards to work with, we jumped in the truck. Grampie maneuvered the truck and trailer, taking up the whole road and driving on the lawn. If there was any way to attract more attention, my grandfather would know how. I couldn't wait to get the heck out of there. Later I found out that he had asked before sending me in—wish I knew that beforehand. We went home, pounded out the old square nails, and patched up the barn with the new boards.

Grampie spent more time telling stories than working. And I listened. They were funny and very elaborate tales of his escapades in life. He had a great memory and shared all the details, often cracking himself up before getting to the point of the story. Then I noticed he would continue, tell me the same story, but add even more to it. He must have had an incredible life!

He told me about the Allagash, the Hoover Dam, and working in the wheat fields in Western Canada. Of swimming underwater at great lengths up the river and fooling people. Of fishing and the tricks he used to get his workers to work faster. He talked as we painted, and we painted a lot! He would always tell me, "Don't be afraid to put more paint on that brush," while watching intently over my shoulder making sure that I was doing it right. Grampie taught me how to work and how to work all day. "To find work," he told me, "You always can do something that someone else needs." And he would continue, "If you go where you can be seen, the people will ask for your help."

I had asked the universe for a teacher. I wanted a spiritual teacher to guide me like I had read about in the books. It took me many years to see that Romeo had been that teacher that I needed at that time. What I wouldn't give to have those precious moments back!

10. Entering the "Real" World

My dreams became a reality when I signed up for my first day of my first wilderness job right out of college. Each weekend for four days at a time, I guided students on wilderness expeditions. We backpacked in the White Mountains of Maine and New Hampshire. On the other days of the week, the students had regular classes in the lodges on campus. I started the job in early November while the cold weather was just beginning to set in.

On my first expedition with the students, I used the only sleeping bag I owned and my backpacking pack which was on the small side. I thought these would be good enough, not considering the group equipment I had to carry. My sleeping bag was a high school graduation gift and at its prime it was rated for 20 degrees. That was six years before so it was well worn and really thin by now!

We had a relatively short hike through the woods on a trail that followed a creek. The creek was dotted with boulders that guided the water to flow in small channels around the base of the rocks. The sound of the water rushing by and the breeze shaking the leaves snuck in between the laughter and voices of the students to soothe my ears. When we arrived at the lean-to built of logs, we began to set up camp for the evening. Rolling out our bags, I noticed mine looked very small compared to the others. Not that I wanted to compare myself, but I got the feeling that either it might be much colder than I anticipated, or that they were over-prepared.

That night as the sun set and the moon rose, the heat slowly escaped my thin sleeping bag. I pulled my head inside the bag, stuffed my clothes in the bottom to keep my feet warm, and tried to block every heat escape I could find. My down vest fit comfortably around my neck just below the hood of my mummy-style sleeping bag. I turned on my side and curled up in the fetal position, trying to keep all the warmth in my core. The sleeping pad beneath me gave some cushion, but didn't keep the cold air from encroaching. The morning sun took it's time rising that day while I waited patiently for the warmth to return. I gathered more awareness around cold weather camping on that trip for sure, although I should have learned this already from my kayaking trip in college!

Over the next few months I worked at the school, transitioning from the cabin life to the wilderness expeditions with students. I watched as they learned and grew and was amazed with what each student had to share. The winter months were cold and challenging. The students would set up a tarp in the shape of an "A." All of the students slept side-by-side like sardines under the tarp with the instructors at each end. There were more times than not where I was outside of the tarp looking up at the crisp night sky from my sleeping bag. I didn't mind though, it was a great view. The stars seem to twinkle more in the crisp, cold air of winter. Often I would wake, buried by snow and sheets of ice from freezing rain and the typical weather in the Northeast.

11. To Florida

I did enjoy my job in the White mountains on the border of Maine and New Hampshire, but I also wanted to experience more wilderness and began the search for my next steps. As a dreamer, I was always looking toward the future and the possibilities. When my internship was complete, I started a whole new adventure, one that I would have never imagined. It began when I agreed to drive my grandparents to Florida in a tiny white Neon with an oversized cargo box attached to the roof. My Grammie sat comfortably in the back seat. Grampie sat in the passenger seat with the road map completely open while looking for "Sylvania." He gave me the route numbers and cities to look for ahead of time. While my grandparents went into the gas station or got out to stretch their legs, I made sure to take a look at the map with my own eyes.

Grampie often pronounced cities differently than I would. And sometimes he would tell me the route numbers in reverse. We drove all the way to Georgia looking for signs that said "Sylvania." Once we hit Georgia I realized what we were actually looking for was "Savannah."

We made it to Florida where we would be renovating a home that my uncle bought so my grandparents would have a warm place to stay during the winter. As part of the renovations, Grampie and I were going to tear the rug out of one of the rooms. Grampie bounced on the floor here and there testing to get a feel for what was underneath the carpet. He said, "Yes, it's rotten." So we got our safety goggles and gloves and began peeling up the carpet, afraid of what we would find. We loosened up where the edges of the carpet met the wall. Inch by inch we pulled that old, smelly carpet back, afraid to look at the damage underneath. When enough was loose, we peeled it back to reveal... a gray floor! It was hard concrete, not rotten at all! My silly grandfather. We sure were relieved and laughed the rest of the night.

It felt so good to sit and listen to my grandfather's stories. He loved to eat in restaurants, so this is where I heard most of the tales from his life. One day over breakfast, he got so into his story, the waitresses had to clean around us. The smell of bleach water filled the air as they wiped down the tables. The mop made a swishing sound behind me while one of the waitresses put the chairs upside down on the tables. They were getting ready to close for the day. Despite what was going on around us, Grampie smiled. With a toothpick held between his pointer finger and thumb and his elbow resting on the table, he waved his hand back and forth along with the story. I was amazed at how he stayed completely focused on the telling of his story. He drew me in. Even though I had heard it before, he stole my attention away from all other distractions.

I sat across the table looking into my grandfather's eyes, bright blue and smiling. His eyes were so youthful, even while his body said otherwise. He led an adventurous life and shared his unique perspectives on the world, and he shared this with me as if he needed someone to hold it for him. It was precious for me to hear the words he spoke, even when I found it hard to believe, or understand.

He told me about working on the Allagash Wilderness Waterway and other rivers in Northern Maine. Standing on logs with nails in his shoes and spinning them under his feet while the logs flowed down the river. He said they would try to see how fast they could get the logs spinning. When he first told me this, I gasped in disbelief. I thought he was so incredible to make up such things. I had a hard time believing it until I saw the pictures of the river drivers with nails extending out the bottom of their shoes who would get on the logs in the river to move them! Maine since the 1600s used the rivers to move logs rather than trucks and roads. And there were people who were out there on the rivers all day making sure the logs didn't get jammed.

Grampie shared all kinds of stories of working in the forest. He said they kept their hair long to cover their face, keeping them warm while they slept. And how they cooked their meals and buried them in the ground to keep them warm overnight. He told me about driving across the country to work in the wheat fields and the "big dam out West" which I later discovered was the Hoover Dam. My heart was filled when hearing how he bought his mother a washing machine with the money he earned on a trip to work out West. She could then turn a crank to agitate and wash the clothes, rather than using the washboard to clean clothes by hand. My great-grandmother ran a business washing and pressing clothes, while my grandfather would ride his bike to deliver the clothes to the neighbors. With this new washing machine, she was able to be more efficient and wash even more clothes for more people.

Grampie and I spent much time working and just as much time taking breaks in the shade. I listened intently as I knew these stories would not be told in this way forever. I committed as much as I could to memory and promised I would share them again someday. What I remember most are those timeless moments we shared together. The laughs, the wonder, and the curiosity stay with me until this day.

When I wasn't working, writing, or sitting for coffee with my grandparents, I was riding the neighbors giant tricycle around the block. The community was small where they lived, and I would go out cruising around the neighborhood. I loved the sun, the breeze in my hair, and watching the silhouette of the palm trees as the sun set.

I spent three weeks in Florida before flying back to Maine. After my return, my uncle flew down to finish the renovations. My plan was to go home to Maine and then fly to Tucson, Arizona for one of the largest gem shows in the world. My friend would be hosting the first annual "Gem and Jam Festival," and I wanted to take part! I didn't want to miss a gathering of friends, live music, and crystals. I bought a one-way ticket from Portland, Maine, and soon was landing in the small Tucson, Arizona airport. My friend Toby arrived to pick me up with his fancy rental car and my journey Out West began.

12. To Tucson

In this whirlwind of excitement I ventured to the desert south-west with the dream of landing an awesome outdoor job. I imagined living an adventurous life by myself in Sedona, Arizona, learning skills and preparing to become a wilderness guide in some of the most awesome places on earth.

The voice on the other end of the phone assured me, "Yes. The school is close enough to Sedona that you can walk there." And of course I believed what the woman on the other end of the phone said. After the Tucson gem show, a friend drove me north to Sedona in a big white Econoline van. I was scheduled for an interview with the dean of the school, but when we arrived he wasn't on campus and no one knew where he was or when he would return. This made me feel uneasy, as we were clearly scheduled and I had come so far for the meeting. I met and talked with several of the office staff and was given a quick tour of the campus. The campus was damp, and there was evidence of recent flooding, yet it was nestled in the beautiful desert and this had been one of the rainiest years on record for the area! The desert was in bloom and it was amazing. People flew in from all over the world to view the desert plants in bloom. Some flowers had not been seen in over 100 years! It was a very special time, and I was happy to be immersed in this thriving desert experience. The colors, the brightness, and the sweet damp smell of the dirt is one that I will never forget.

I accepted the job and made my way toward the next chapter in my life. Partly I felt nervous to learn a new job where I knew no one, but mostly I was excited to be in such an amazing place with a job that sounded very fun and also fulfilling. The red rock canyons and formations were literally my new backyard.

Upon my arrival, I came to find out that the only road to the school had flooded from the rain, so it was hard to get on and off campus. I was dropped off, shown my room in the girls dorm and set off to "realize my dream." It wasn't long that I realized this job was not what I thought it would be, or what I was told it would be.

I had a prepaid cell phone with me for emergencies. If I wanted to use it, I had to add calling minutes with a credit card before making calls. I felt so alone that I dialed my sisters and my mom at least once each day, but usually even more than that. The job I had been promised wasn't nearly what it turned out to be. The hourly head counts of the students and being a "dorm Mother" weren't mentioned in the initial conversations. I was told I would be leading white water rafting and rock climbing trips. I wondered, "What happened with the ropes course and backpacking that I was hired for?"

The day came for the adventure that was promised. I woke to my alarm at 4 a.m. and began packing the van with coolers full of food. Stumbling around the darkness, I checked each dorm and woke only the students who would be traveling with me that day. They packed and we loaded the van. I was the only teacher and adult on this particular trip, and we had a six-hour drive ahead. We stopped at a gas station to have a quick break and grab some snacks before heading up the canyon.

The teenagers were all asleep as I drove the van up the winding roads toward Globe, Arizona. The roads brought us up out of the valley just as the sun's rays began peaking over the mountains. It had been raining for weeks, so the cactus flowers and plants were bright green and in full bloom. The sun warmed the earth and the moisture escaped in misty vapor that rose. It was an incredible moment to witness. With excitement, I woke the students so they could open their eyes to the scenery. The next thing I knew, they were throwing pennies and shoes in my direction; they were bouncing off the windshield in front of me. "I'll play your favorite music," I said, hoping to instill some inspiration. So we listened to rap and drove up the winding canyon road, the towering saguaro cactus watching over us.

After a long drive we arrived at the Salt River, ready for wetsuits. We slid the raft into the river and began to float down with the current. The students wanted to "swamp the teacher" of course, so it was quite a battle for me to stay in the raft. We had lunch, rafted again, and then loaded up the van for the ride home.

I felt exhausted, emotionally, physically, and mentally. A large cup of cheap coffee would assist me over the next six hours driving in the dark back down the canyon. Circling the city lights of Phoenix, we headed into the final stretch until finally arriving back at the school in the dark quiet solitude of the desert.

After unpacking and cleaning out the van, my supervisor asked me to be on security that evening. My thoughts turned over in my tired mind. I had been up since four o'clock in the morning and worked an entire 18-hour shift with no assistance. That moment was my breaking point. Mustering the courage, my voice rattled a clear "no" as I headed back toward my room. I was on salary pay, which seemed like a good idea at first, but putting my best forward for 18-hour shifts and 80-hour work weeks was too much. The jobs weren't the same as I had been told, I had to take a stand. I needed rest if I were going to be present for this job and for these students.

That night I made my way to my room. Exhausted, I lay on my bed and slept for a long time. To this day I am not sure how long I slept but I didn't get up to make sure the students brushed their teeth and I didn't get up for any head counts. I slept and woke up, staying mostly delirious and in a dream state for several days. Finally, I prayed, "What can I do?" This was supposed to be my dream job. I thought this was going to be awesome. But the reality was much different than I ever could have imagined.

I felt so alone and lost. A heart-wrenching disappointment filled my body as shame creeped in. Anger bubbled up for not seeing this ahead of time and for ignoring the warning signs. I sat on my bed afraid to leave my room. My body frozen with fear, I sat quietly and tried to read. Resting my body, I listened deeply to my quietest thoughts. Every so often there would be a gentle knock at my door, and when I opened it to look out, I'd find a styrofoam container left for me. A meal. Someone here did care.

My adventurous spirit led me to spending days trying to walk to Sedona through the desert. Over the hills I ventured, hoping that at the top of the next hill I would be in Sedona. Reaching the top of the next hill, disappointment would fill me when it appeared so far away. So many hills to travel up and over and down. It just wasn't possible to do in one day. I felt lied to. I felt used. And I wasn't going to take it. I had to do something different. I decided to leave the job and not return.

There was one teacher who I had become friends with who had a car on campus. On his next day off he and another friend I had made drove me into the town of Sedona to drop me off. I found the cheapest hotel room in the whole town. They dropped me off with my backpack, crystals, and replica of a Mayan tablet under my arm. As their laughs left and the tiny light blue car drove off, I found myself alone once again. My room for the night had an amazing view of coffee pot rock. I showered, lay in bed and slept a very deep sleep.

In the morning, I felt different and realized I was scared. Not having a job or a car, or even any friends nearby, and I was far from home and my family. How would I support myself from here? But I also felt a sense of freedom, and I felt proud for standing up for myself.

Sipping a warm cup of coffee from my stainless steel mug in the cool shadowy morning, I watched as the light of the day began. The blazing colors, reds and oranges, emanated from the rocks, a reflection of the glow from the sun. I walked around to check out the area. There was a crystal shop next door, a Thai food restaurant, and the public library close by.

My plan was to walk to the library and search for a job on the library computers. I walked to the library and went inside. It was quiet with the subtle sounds of fingers on the keys of the keyboard typing. To reserve a spot to use the internet I had to sign up on the clipboard. When a computer became available, I had exactly one half hour to complete my search, before the computer would sign me out for the next person's turn. If it wasn't too busy, sometimes I could sign up again, but there was limited time to do everything. I would check my email quickly, and then browse the outdoor jobs listed hoping to find a good match for me.

I sent my outdoor resume and cover letter to every job that looked interesting. I wanted the job to cover food and housing, or at least part of that, and to give me great outdoor and leadership experience. I had wanted to become a mountain guide, to climb high peaks, travel across glaciers, and see alpine lakes. So whatever could get me closer to that dream would be awesome! But I also had to pay the student loans that I had borrowed to get the degree. I was not aware that the amount I borrowed would be so hard to pay off with the type of jobs I was eligible for.

I stayed in Sedona for almost a week at the hotel. It was beautiful, spiritual, and amazing, yet I had never felt so alone. Sitting at a Mexican restaurant eating nachos and writing in my journal, I dreamed of an epic life. My future was unplanned and open, what did I want to do? What would I be able to create? Just then my Tracfone began to buzz on the table. It was an old friend calling. He invited me to come visit him in Prescott, Arizona, which was just over an hour drive away. He happened to have a friend driving through Sedona from Flagstaff, just north of me, and his friend had offered to give me a ride down to Prescott. It felt like the universe heard my wishes, and had made arrangements for the next stage of my life.

On the back deck, or rather a concrete slab at the back door of my friend's home in Prescott, Arizona, I paced back and forth while listening to the man on the other end of the telephone. I felt excited and nervous about the unknown and possibilities of a new job. I was also aware that I didn't want to fall into the same trap that I had just left. What if I make a wrong decision? What if I don't ask enough questions, or the right questions? With my prepaid cell phone, I was able to do preliminary interviews while I lived on the road. Hitchhiking with a small backpack of my meager belongings, I felt a freedom I had never known before and this job sounded promising. The job was located in Colorado, in the Four Corners area. We talked several times before I decided to trust my gut and go for it.

I traded an oil change for the ride, because for some reason the trains didn't run that way, or the other option would take days by bus. It was about a nine-hour drive, and we listened to the Grateful Dead "...and she takes her fan and throws it in the lion's den...Terrapin, I can't figure out, Terrapin, if it's the end or beginning..." And we sang all the way there. It felt like everything was aligned just perfectly and I was off again to realize my dream. But I was about to embark on an adventure that I hadn't been prepared for.

13. Colorful Colorado & The High Desert

found myself at the front desk of the Blue Sky Motel, the owner, an Australian man of many jokes, had just changed the name from the Blue Fox Motel. He explained that he didn't want people to think it was a rent-by-the-hour kind of place. I ordered a pizza for delivery, hung up the phone, and fell backwards onto the bed with a sigh. The room smelled musty but it was cheap and was a good place to sleep for a night. I was nervous and visibly shaking as I thought about the job training ahead, but I felt like things were moving forward for me. This would be another adventure! With no car, no place to live, and no friends within hours of me, that lonely feeling crept in again. But I had finally arrived at my first "official" job after college. I had no idea what lay ahead of me now.

The area just a few hours north of Durango was beautiful. Surrounded by mountains and mesas, with the desert just to the south, I had much to explore. I almost signed a lease on a small cabin in Placerville, near Telluride, but I decided if I was going to pay rent, I would much rather buy a car and pay the lease. That way I'd be free to explore the western states.

I drove the blue soft cover Jeep into the dealer. It was a sunny day, springtime. The air in Colorado is a bit thinner and less humid than Maine. "Are you thinking of trading this one in?" "Well actually no, this is my friend's Jeep." A woman from my training had let me borrow her Jeep for the week while she was working in the field. We had been hired for opposite shifts and since the shifts were eight days on followed by six days off, she wouldn't be needing it for several days. A gold Astro van caught my eye and after test driving it, I seriously considered it. I needed something that I could live in, that I could stretch out comfortably and sleep in the back, and that would take me on the back roads.

Then the dealer came out with a car that had just been freshly detailed. The Mazda Tribute was just a few years old. As a leased car, the mileage was pretty low. I wanted it! I put the seats down in the back, climbed in, and stretched out. Yes this would be ideal. I fit perfectly and would be able to sleep comfortably. It had a moonroof, 4-wheel drive, and it smelled new (which I think is that new car smell they spray in cars so you want to buy them.) So I called my mom and talked it over to see what she thought. I had just barely started a new job, and I had never leased a car before, but I was all the way out in Colorado, way far from home and from anyone I knew. I wanted and needed something reliable.

I left the dealership headed toward the Best Western where I had been staying. I asked the universe to give me a sign if this was the car to buy or not. My flip phone buzzed in my hand, it was the dealer texting me at exactly 3:33 p.m. I thought, wow, it must be a sign because the timing is exactly perfect. I had been in my hotel looking at the replica of the Mayan tablet and playing with my mini collection of crystals trying to figure out if it was a good idea or not. And soon I was so excited, I felt a freedom well up inside of me, because I knew that if I had wheels, I could visit my friends who lived somewhat near, or at least nine hours away. So I went back in and leased my very first car which became my home.

During my time off I found all the free campgrounds near me and places I could shower. The drive through the mountains was amazing and from where I worked, I often traveled over Red Mountain Pass and Lizard Head Pass. These were two of the most scenic drives in Colorado. This was going to be an epic year!

14. Seeking Treasure on the Mountain

My love for crystal hunting, still strong, led me to climbing Mount Antero in the Collegiate Peaks in Colorado. The few hand tools I had, rattled in the small pack on my back. I climbed higher and higher, rounding the mountain through the forest and up in elevation to where the trees increasingly grew smaller and further apart. Scrambling over large gray boulders and mounds of rock and sand, I witnessed the peaks of jagged mountains as they extended into the skyline. The trees grew smaller and smaller until they completely faded out, leaving me walking on bare rock and sand. And still I went higher.

My destination was the highest mineral collecting locality in North America. I had heard stories of minerals such as phenakite and aquamarine being dug there and I just had to see for myself. Turning to look back down the trail, I could see the trees were just a speck in the distance and the mountain peaks loomed ahead. I got an eerie feeling as dark clouds built on the horizon, eventually moving toward each other before colliding.

In the case of a lightning storm, which was about 100% likely at this point, I knew the safest place was far below me in the trees. As the sky grew darker and darker, I walked faster and faster heading downhill towards those tiny dots of trees I had passed hours ago. Forgetting about the crystal hunt, my mind and actions focused on safety. The clouds built higher and crashed into each other. The hair stood up on the back on my neck as the loud cracks and booms echoed through the peaks. Where I stood all felt eerily still, yet the world around me was quickly closing in.

With each rumble of thunder I could feel the vibration through the earth and I pushed my legs harder in a full sprint down the mountain. With every ounce of energy I could muster, I headed straight for the tree line. I could smell the ozone in the air, and could feel that electrical feeling moving through my body. The trees got closer and then, with another crash, the rain fell like buckets of water being poured over me. And then came the hail. The rain fell as hail pelted me from above, bouncing and collecting on the trail in front of me.

As soon as I hit the trees I realized that the tools in my backpack were metal. Ripping my backpack off my back, I threw it as far as I could at the same time hurrying into a lightning drill position. Crouching with bum to heels, and bent over, the lightning struck nearby trees. I mumbled to myself, "I am not ready to die. I am not ready yet." I held this thought knowing inside of me that this might be my last moment. I tried to smell every last smell, to see every last color, to absorb as much as I could from that moment of living, just in case that was my last. Just in case that would be my very last moment to breathe on this earth. Moment to moment I prayed that the lightning would not hit me, as I heard the limbs of trees fall and saw fires spark around me.

Soon the wind slowed and the rain softened. The thunder moved to the other side of the mountain and flashes of lightning dimmed and finally passed. I emerged from the trees and took a big breath of air. There was the smell of smoke in the air and flames in the distance. I found my backpack and as I put it on, the sun lit up a rainbow over my head. Several hours later, back toward the base of the mountain my cell phone had reception so I called my mom just to say, "Hi." The treasure I found on that mountain that day was to live every moment as your last. Let the people in your life know that you appreciate them and love them because you never know when your last moment together might be.

I loved my job as a Backcountry Field Instructor. The work weeks consisted of eight days on followed by six days off work. This fed my adventurous lifestyle and allowed me to travel around Colorado and the surrounding areas to explore during my cycles off. Sometimes those eight days in the field felt very long.

After a long shift out in the high desert west of Montrose, Colorado, my coworkers and I had an old Suburban on the muddy road and were heading back to town for our six days off. The snow had melted, and it was raining, adding slickness to the mess. We drove out of the desert happy to be off shift. I had a week-long vacation so I would have the following three weeks off.

Driving on the muddy roads we played music, sang, and worked our way out of the back-road maze. Soon we began to fish tail and the driver couldn't maintain it, so we slipped off the road ever so slightly. Slightly maybe, but it was enough to get us really stuck. We quickly made a plan to push the Suburban out. One of my coworkers got in the driver's seat and two of us pushed from the back. The mud was flung up by the tires, slapping us in the face as we pushed with all our strength. We would slip a bit to this side or that, but didn't manage to get any further. All three of us rotated taking turns driving and then pushing, getting completely covered in mud in the process. We were tired and we were stuck. No one had driven by, and we didn't expect anyone to as we were way out and far from any tarred roads.

So we sat on the side of the road; the Minister, Louisiana Boy, and I. The Minister began to sing, "So rock me momma like a wagon wheel, rock me momma any way you feel…" and we all started to sing. Then he began to pray. He said that was his way, and I was thinking, "How can praying get us out of the mud? What can God do for us now?" And within a few short minutes, a truck came up the muddy road, pulled up beside us, and two men asked if we needed any help. With their truck and some chains, our Suburban was out of the mud pretty quickly and we were on our way!

We returned to the base really late to complete the paper-work from the field. We filled out reports for every student's progress. It was always the last thing to complete before the shift officially ended. Filing the last papers in their proper folders, I breathed a sigh of relief for that long week to be complete. I then slept at a friend's house nearby. Early in the morning, just as the sun rose and with only a few blinks of sleep, I had to walk to the airport. With my heavy dirty bag and no time for a shower, I checked in for my flight back home to Maine.

I hopped on the plane with a bag full of clothes that I had been wearing and carrying for 16 days now that were completely covered in mud. I sat down cautiously next to a businessman. The plane was small, a puddle jumper, that would take us from Montrose, Colorado to another small airport and then finally to Denver. I was very conscious of the stench I brought with me, and also noted how inside the plane there's not much air circulation. So if someone's perfume had bothered me in the past, oh boy this must be awful for those around me. Shrinking slowly in my seat I was afraid to move too much. "Did they notice?" They had to! If only I could have had time for a shower. The mud was dried and crusted by now and broke off in flakes around me. I was careful not to get too close to anyone...however I was in a pickle. It was warm on the plane, and I didn't dare to take my mud encrusted rain jacket off as I believed that was trapping in most of the smell. In my mind I was going back and forth, well this is natural, what if we all just didn't wear deodorant?

But my goodness, I had been sweating and hiking for 16 days and in the mud. This is going to be a long couple of flights back home to Maine. Meanwhile we heard an announcement and had to make an emergency landing. The airplane had developed a problem during the flight. An unexpected detour had us landing in a small town somewhere in the midwest.

Once we landed, I went right in and stood in line to wait to speak with the attendants behind the desk. They were scrambling trying to accommodate all of the business people and get them to their destinations. I waited patiently, actually feeling pretty mellow and curious about how this adventure would unfold. When it was my turn I approached the counter. And once again I became conscious of my presence, and tried to ignore it. There were no flights going to Portland, Maine until the next day. I wanted so badly to get home and back to the ocean, however they offered me a hotel for the night and a meal voucher so I gladly accepted. What a gift!

I hopped on the shuttle to the hotel, got a free room, washed all my clothes in the washer and dried them. The warm water from the shower felt good on my sore muscles and the mud slowly disintegrated. I loaded my hair with conditioning cream and brushed all the knots out of the tangled mess. I grabbed a chicken BLT at the restaurant and settled in for one of the best night's sleep in a very long time.

Feeling refreshed and ready, I made my way back to Maine, grateful for the gift of the clean clothes, fresh food, a shower, and a refreshed mind. Of course hopping on the next plane, I felt way more at ease and social than I had the day before.

15. The Instructor Course

I was closing in on a year working as a backcountry field instructor with adjudicated youth in a wilderness program. These were students who were sent to the program by the court or Department of Human Services. The wilderness program was considered a residential treatment program, although all of it took place several hours from base out in the desert. Sticking around for this length of time gave me experience and led me to be one of the most senior instructors in the field. It wasn't easy work in any capacity. We hiked everyday throughout the year in Colorado in hot, buggy summers and wet, frigid winters.

All supplies were carried in our backpacks and fires were made using primitive skills. Mountain sage and juniper were turned into bow drill fire kits. Meals were prepared on the open flames in a single pot. We gathered water from small creeks and carried the jugs miles over the desert while fueling ourselves with what we called "gut bomb," "bear grease," and gorp. These were meals made of pasta, sauce, and cheese or grits, butter, and bacon. We only carried one-pot meals, and ate the same meals and snacks over and over each week, but the food wasn't the hardest part.

I worked with kids who said they wanted to kill me. They lashed out, yelled, punched the earth and we, as instructors and guides, would hold space for all that even if it was midnight or four in the morning. As the months went on I felt this taking a toll on me mentally and physically. I began to feel a strong pull to change my lifestyle.

My desire to work with people who really wanted to be out in the wilderness crept into my conscious thoughts. I found myself daydreaming of being with people who wanted to be leaders in their communities, or who wanted to guide others in the wilderness. It began to take the forefront of my mind and spilled out into my journal entries. Following that desire, I flipped through the images in the NOLS catalogue imagining the possibilities. When I felt exhausted and had given all I had to give to wilderness therapy, I finally made the decision to take a new path.

The decision didn't cause immediate change, yet that is when I began looking for it. Sitting in the quiet stillness at the local library between shifts at my wilderness therapy job, I pulled together all of my leadership hours from high school until present. Remembering the mountains and routes I climbed and the technical and group skills required for each, I documented everything. Digging through my past, I unearthed every bit of leadership training and practice I had, every trip I led, every group I guided, and every personal achievement in the realm of outdoors and leadership. Seeking out past NOLS instructors, I interviewed them to find out about the organization and their personal experiences to quench my curiosity about what it was like to be an instructor. Being real with where I was with my own technical skills, decision making, and experience was clearly important. This document came out to be almost 35 pages long! I printed it out, organized the pages of the application, and put everything carefully into a large yellow envelope. I pulled up to the local post office in Colorado knowing that dropping this in the mailbox could change the direction of my life. With butterflies in my stomach and fingers crossed, I sent the application off.

Several weeks went by and I carried on as usual day in and day out until finally, the day came when I received a letter back from NOLS. The envelope shook as I tried to steady my hand. I slid my finger under the sealed envelope. Pulling out the pages I held my breath as I read the first few sentences. I let out a huge sigh of relief (for a quick moment anyway) when I realized I was accepted to join the National Outdoor Leadership School Southwest Mountain Instructor Course! This, I would find out later, would be a 35-day nail-biting intensive interview.

The days passed and the course drew nearer. With each day, my excitement grew and so did my anticipation. I had decided to begin with the Women's Rock and Leadership Course to help ease my way into the Southwest Mountain Instructor Course. This would also build my confidence on the rock and strengthen my skills with gear placement and anchor building. It was an opportunity to meet other women who would be on the instructor course (IC) and to build a bond and support system that would carry us through the 35-day course. There weren't many women in this field at the time; we made up only one-fourth of the total students in the course. This "pre-course" turned out to be one of the most influential courses I have ever taken. The course strengthened teaching, leadership, and technical skills based on gender learning styles, and it was a lot of fun!

The full expedition began immediately following the pre-course. As cars drove into the dirt parking lot of the Tucson, Arizona base, more and more students made themselves known. With this my confidence began to dwindle—everyone seemed to have so much experience and skill. I shrugged it off and kept as focused as I could as we packed and prepared for the journey ahead. I packed and unpacked my pack many times trying to find the lightness and balance. We calculated precisely how much food to bring based on pounds of food per person per day, then planned our meals and weighed our food rations accordingly. Fully loaded with personal and group gear, our packs were weighed and we headed out to the Aldo Leopold Wilderness and the Gila Wilderness in New Mexico for our 19-day backpacking section.

We practiced guiding the group through the woods, sometimes through burnt and recovering forest. Often the Instructor Team, who we called the "I-Team," would sit quietly observing as they waited for the "Leader of the Day" to organize and make decisions for the travel group. This was to help us learn the most we could in a relatively short period. And this was so frustrating at times!

We had been traveling several miles when we couldn't find the trail: there were too many fallen trees criss-crossing our path and we couldn't see our way. Scouting ahead, I couldn't find the next blaze that marked the trail. Our instructor calmy posed the question, "When was the last time you saw a trail marker?" Everyone stopped in silence to think. No one could recall the last marker. As seasoned hikers from different parts of the world, we should remember the last trail marker. We tried communicating with each other what we could remember. Our

Instructor left it at that and left it up to us to make a group decision. I remember feeling my own frustration, for at this point I had become pretty tired. The hike wasn't easy, uphill and lots of scrambling, as well as constant decisions, briefs, debriefs, and "teachable moments." I was content to hike and enjoy the view of the wilderness, but we did have to learn to pay attention. The Instructors allowed us to make mistakes and wrong turns. They let us struggle in different situations to see how we responded to stress. We were encouraged to explore our options to make more informed decisions. We were encouraged to expand our awareness of potential situations and solutions. These situations we encountered were opportunities to experience these types of moments in preparation for leading others. During the debrief at the end of that hiking section, we talked about what happened and how to make it better, easier, or safer next time.

On this course I found myself scrambling up talus slopes, one step forward, then sliding one step back. Gathering strength I'd climb up again a few yards, and then slide back down. It was challenging mentally and physically to experience such slow progress forward. My mind wandered over so many questions: "How would I travel safely with a group on such terrain? When does a group travel close together? When does the group spread out and travel further apart? When is it appropriate to cut across and when would a group travel straight up?" My mind also churned with, "When will this be over?"

The focus was on safety and risk management while traversing and climbing in some of the most incredible mountains and canyons. This terrain was obviously a lot different than what I was used to in the Northeast where I grew up, but each lesson helped me to understand how the earth moved, and to be able to see potential hazards and how to deal with those effectively.

I could take everything I was learning and apply it to any terrain. That was the focus, so we weren't being trained to guide in a specific area, but to teach others how to be a leader in all areas of life, and not only to apply the curriculum to life in the wilderness, but also back at home. That is why I was so drawn to NOLS as a school, and I wanted to do my very best on this training. I was there to learn the most I could possibly learn and this was the most experiential and "safe" way to explore.

All skills, hard and soft, were scrutinized under the eyes of the Instructor Team. They were observing our technical skills as well as our personalities, habits, and communications skills. The Instructor Team, backed by experience and training, were looking at how we presented the curriculum, our teaching skills and our expedition behavior. They viewed and challenged our ability to solve problems while keeping the group safe, happy, and engaged in learning.

The month-long instructor course itself was intense. We were in the Gila Wilderness for a 19-day technical backpacking section practicing teaching the NOLS curriculum. The instructors pushed us with long hiking days until we were tired physically and mentally. Then they had us cook and teach to see how we would respond and function while tired and under a little stress. We would get up at four in the morning and hike down a canyon with little water, then up and over a mountain, along a ridge and back down where we would have a first aid scenario and then cook dinner. That would be followed by a class held in the dark as the night grew late. We had to demonstrate our ability to think and solve problems while managing risks in the backcountry, despite the circumstances. The terrain was beautiful, the people interesting and yet my attitude was challenged. I felt a weird mix of exhaustion and inspiration.

Getting toward the end of the backpacking section, my instructor pulled me aside for our check-in and evaluation meeting and said, "Well, Jaclyn, you do have a lot of flair. And people seem to like you." I couldn't tell if this was an insult or encouragement. She seemed surprised that people liked my personality. The flair and creative character were encouraged for instructors at NOLS, luckily.

After the backpacking section we moved on to "climb camp." The sun warmed my face as it peeked over the giant boulders on my morning jog. Moving along the dirt trails around the ancient granite in Cochise Stronghold outside of Tucson, Arizona, the familiar smell of the warming desert after a cool night filled my nose.

Practicing yoga and breathing to open my mind and body in the presence of amazing granite cliffs lifted my spirits. Following our small group breakfast, we would drive, park, and hike to the climb for the day. I was so psyched to be living this way: outdoors in the wilderness, in a small community, with beauty and adventure around me. I was ecstatic to be moving toward my dreams. Ten years in the making and here I was living the reality that was once just pictures in magazines and ideas in my imagination.

My climbing instructors were very creative and would develop activities for me to do so they could gauge my problem-solving abilities and stretch the creativity in my thinking. It is these skills you need to depend on when you run into situations in the backcountry.

One instructor had me placing climbing gear in challenging terrains, or he'd add restrictions to the equipment I could use. He wanted to see what I could do and how I would respond. There are passive and active types of gear used as protection when rock climbing. Passive gear has no moving parts and can be wedged into a crack. If the climber were to fall, the gear would remain jammed in the rock, catching the climbing rope attached to the climber and shortening the fall. The active climbing gear involves mechanical or moving parts. When the trigger on the device is pulled, it becomes smaller and therefore will fit into a crack. When the trigger is released, the gear expands and becomes wedged into the crack. If a force is acted on the placed gear in a downward motion, such as when a climber falls, the gear stays wedged and the climber is stopped from falling further. These are temporarily placed and will be removed once the climbers are done with their climb. Most climbers use a mix of active and passive gear in this type of climbing, traditional climbing, or trad for short.

"Cams" are active gear. Some cams are smaller than half of my thumb. Yet some are extremely large for placement in larger cracks. The instructor took me over to a ledge that was about five feet wide. There were big boulders, taller than me, set on this ledge. It was windy up there, the wind caught the wisps of my hair that had come loose from my ponytail beneath my helmet. The cliff and boulders were old granite, a beautiful peachy color, yet it was abrasive and scratched my skin. I was afraid where I was. Looking down, it was a long way to the bottom! The instructor tied me in to an anchor, yet the rope had plenty of slack so I could move around. He was also tied in as he began to give the instructions.

The task was to build an anchor that we could hang a rope to rappel down, and then be able to climb back up. I thought that was reasonable and sounded like a fun challenge. Then he handed me the largest cams available (and they had some big ones!) to add to my rack of gear. These cams were bigger than my two fists together and as they are made of metal, were also quite heavy. I clipped them to the sling draped over my shoulder with my other gear. Scrambling around on my belly because my legs were shaking, I dragged these oversized cams with me. They kept getting caught up in the small nooks as I squeezed through and around the rocks and boulders. However, I managed to build the anchor, but had to access my creativity and patience in the process. Double checking and triple checking the knots, the back ups, and the locks, I knew it was ready. The final test was to put the anchor to use. I clipped in with my instructor backing me up...and sure enough, soon I was hanging from my anchor out over a cliff. Never did I run across a situation where I needed to build an anchor like that again, but from that experience I learned to look at a challenge, and to see more options.

By the end of the 35-day backpacking and climbing course, I learned a ton more, had fun, and explored amazing places. Yet I still had the repeating nagging thoughts in the back of my mind: "Am I going to be good enough?" "Do I know enough?" "Do I have what it takes?" "Is this for me?" These thoughts bubbled up from my subconscious making me feel uneasy and unsure. I found myself constantly trying to squash these thoughts or ignore them. These were familiar thoughts to me, and feelings that were present in all situations in my life, yet they became super amplified during this training.

Back at base we celebrated with a good old-fashioned bar-beque and pool party. My instructors gave me the official job of "Party Planner." I was responsible for the elements of the celebration for the completion of the course. We had a scavenger hunt, a pinata, a barbeque, games, and swimming. This was the best after spending 35 days in the backcountry. However, even through all the fun, I didn't fully let go of the reason why I was there, not even during this celebration. I was still nervous about landing myself a contract. It was rare to be offered work right after the IC, but I was hopeful despite the background thoughts and entertaining the ideas of what I would do if I didn't get hired.

The Instructor Team called the students in one by one to the Map Room. The Arizona sun was shining warm and bright on this early May day. My body was shaking with anticipation as each student went into the house and came out one by one, some shared their experience and some did not. Mostly it was silent. Waiting until the second to last, I sat in the sun journaling out my thoughts and feelings. I was trying to let go of the feelings of "not being good enough," and turning over the scenarios in my mind. Did I really do my best?

"Jaclyn," I heard, snapping me out of my daydream. The Instructor Team was calling me in. All three instructors seemed relaxed and happy, which was a little bit opposite of what I was experiencing at that moment. The room was lit by afternoon sun illuminating the glossy framed maps that hung on the wall. I took a seat in the empty rocking chair and tried to come across like I was "cool" even as the chair squeaked when I sat down. Each sound in the room seemed amplified with my anxiety of what the I-Team would say. The truth was that I wasn't feeling "cool." My heart was beating so hard that I was shaking and sweating. The clock ticking, the squeak of the chair, the water dripping in the kitchen sink, all echoed through my mind. "Just breathe," I kept reminding myself. Each member of the I-Team took their turn sharing what they thought I did well, what my high points were, and reflections on how I presented my skills. I got so intent on listening to what they were saying, that the sound of the dripping faucet didn't bother me anymore.

Each instructor from the I-Team gave clear, positive suggestions. The feedback was relevant for further growth as a Wilderness Instructor and also for me as a human. Hearing their opinions was a great relief because I realized that I had learned so much already! Everything shared with me were things that if I implemented, would help me in my life. Whether I had a contract or not, or whether I even continued to work as a Wilderness Instructor or not, what they shared with me held so much value. I am still grateful for the honest and clear support that came through their genuine responses and their desire to help me to become the best person that I could become.

After all was shared from both sides, I was fortunate to be one of the few to be offered a contract right out of the instructor course. I was so ecstatic my heart jumped in my chest. It beat so hard and loud, it pushed all the blood to my head in a rush. Bubbling with energy, I didn't know what to do, so I accepted the contract then ran outside and jumped in the pool with all my clothes on! With a big splash, I hit the water yelling "Yessssss!" My excitement must have echoed through the canyons.

Looking to my future, I wanted to work in the caving programs as an instructor, as those were some of my most favorite expeditions. The technical skills I picked up from the rock climbing sections could be applied to many situations in vertical and technical caving. Exploring the unseen underground world was fascinating, it especially filled my love for minerals and crystals.

After leaving the Instructor Course, I set off on a mission to learn as much about caves as I could. If I wanted to be a caving instructor, I knew I needed to find out as much as I could and to visit as many caves as possible.

Leaving Tucson, I headed west across the desert. My idea was to stop at every cave I could find from there on out and to learn as much about them as I could. I went to the library and researched cave locations, types of caves, how different caves formed, wet caves, dry caves, and cave formations. I read about cave rescues, caves that only scientists were allowed to go into, and animal adaptations for survival in the darkness of the cave environment. It was all absolutely fascinating. I was fortunate to visit caves in the middle of nowhere on my travels west toward Santa Cruz, California. These were small and rather "undeco-rated" compared to what I saw in New Mexico. But I read about a marble cave in Oregon that I put on my list of "must sees."

16. Solo

Left alone in my friend's home, sipping iced Nestlé Café with almond milk and eating fresh strawberries, I typed the papers for my graduate credits that I had elected to take during my NOLS Instructor course. Studying risk management and decision-making in the wilderness gave me a new perspective on the role of a wilderness instructor. Studying and writing about the experience helped me absorb more of this understanding. I decided to skip the Memorial Day parade because I wanted to finish writing my papers before getting back on the road again.

Watching as my friends pulled out of the driveway, I questioned my decision. Maybe I should do what everyone else is doing and take some time to just enjoy and celebrate. But I quickly went back to the desktop and the lighted screen. My fingers moved quickly over the keys putting thoughts into words. My desire to finish and submit these papers before going back to my small SUV and living on the road was driving the quickness and organization in which I worked.

While writing each day, I made sure to maintain my routine so I could be as efficient and clear as possible. Rolling out of bed early to greet the sun my day began with stretching and soothing my body with yoga and meditation practice on the back porch. The warm California sun warmed my cheeks as I checked in to calm my body and nourish my spirit. Then a quick breakfast of fresh local berries and an iced coffee with almond milk and off to work I went, typing.

I dialed my flip phone to say hello to my family back at home in Maine. There was a party that I knew I was missing. When I called, the music in the background made it hard to hear, everyone was dancing and celebrating my grandparents' anniversary. My family passed the phone around so I could speak to everyone and wished my grandparents a happy anniversary. I could only imagine my grandparents on the dance floor! That must have been fun. My family sure did enjoy the family gatherings and celebrations and I missed being there for sure.

Meanwhile, I was inside the house pounding iced coffee and almond milk while finishing up my graduate papers. My heart felt heavy with questions. "Was this the right decision?" The words rolled through my mind like the ocean waves I heard in the distance. I was soaking up the vibrancy of the greenest grass I had ever seen, picking berries from bushes as tall as trees, the warm ocean breeze kissing my cheeks, climbing, caving, backpacking, and living the adventurous life I had dreamed of. But I started to feel like I was alone, very alone. There wasn't anyone sharing this journey with me and even speaking about it wasn't really sharing the magnificence of what I felt or saw. It was just me and my experience, and actually, that part was pretty incredible.

When I left Santa Cruz, I headed north on State Route 1 which follows the coast of California. I was driving to Idaho and a job interview to see if I might be interested in working there.

My sunroof was open, my hair blowing wildly and my voice lost in the wind as I tried my best to sing to the music playing through my ipod.

I was on my own time the whole way, stopping to enjoy the water and views in places that called me, and staying as long as I enjoyed. I camped on the sandy beaches beneath the palm trees at the state parks on my way to a pit stop at Oregon Caves National Monument. This seemed like a good opportunity to talk with as many cavers as I could. I stopped at the local library to read up on caves in the area. The marble caves were amazing. The tour guide brought us on a narrow path that wound its way through the wet caves. The marble was damp, and I could hear the echoing drips as the water droplets fell from the ceiling. The air had a musty, cool quality to it and the formations were still growing and changing. It was amazing to be inside a cave that had so much sound and movement. The cave formations were still changing. The caves in New Mexico were mostly very dry. I am so happy to have stopped and enjoyed Oregon before driving east to Idaho.

Driving through Idaho, I noticed similarities in the types of high desert plants I passed as the plants in the Southwest, but also many differences. The mountains were rugged and the colors and jagged shapes of the rocks made me feel like I was a visitor on another planet. I imagined the moon having the same colored rocks. I drove by the Sawtooth Mountains, along a slowly winding creek with an old wooden fence that ran along its edge.

I was in Idaho for hands-on training in the wilderness with about 20 other instructors. The weekend expedition was an interview for a job working with students in the wilderness. We would be teaching urban and wilderness survival skills. Our group walked through the high desert. The air was a little more humid than the Southwest and had a sweet smell. After a day and a night in the backcountry, I noticed a slight twinge of a headache. The instructors told me to drink more water, so I did. But they insisted we drink more and more water. At times we would be called to gather in a circle to finish drinking the water in the bottle. We had to alert an instructor, who would watch as we flipped the bottle upside down to indicate we had finished all of the water.

Soon I became dizzy and very nauseous. I was having a hard time walking and thinking. The instructors tried talking to me, but I felt awful. I do pretty well in the desert and the heat, but was having a really hard time functioning on this particular trip. I sat down, too dizzy to stand. I remember feeling like the instructors thought I was pretending, or just weak as they drilled me with questions. I didn't want to do this anymore, I just wanted to lay down and sleep. I was peeing a lot! But somehow I still felt dehydrated. They told me to drink more water, but I felt full of water. Someone sitting close to me gave me some salted sunflower seeds and I sucked the salt off them and spit them out. Slowly I regained my sense of self. We determined after returning to the base, that I had hyponatremia from drinking too much water. This had washed all of the nutrients out of my body making me unable to function properly. It was an awful experience, and scary looking back on it. I decided that was a clear sign to leave Idaho.

The next thing I knew I was on an airplane leaving Salt Lake City, Utah on a flight to Charlotte, North Carolina. I spent three weeks in the forest in the Blue Ridge Mountains. I sure did miss the wide open skies as North Carolina had thick, lush trees with gigantic angel-shaped leaves. Although I loved the lush forest, the streams, and greenery, I missed the wide open skies of the West. Upon completing my contract, I flew back to Utah and back to my home on wheels. I was happy to be driving my Tribute north toward Jackson, Wyoming where I would spend time with friends rafting, canoeing, swimming, and playing horseshoes.

Finally in mid-July, I made it to Lander, Wyoming! This is where I began my first contract for NOLS and guided my first 30-day expedition in the Wind River Range.

17. Living the Dream

am brought back from my early morning thoughts by the sound of laughter echoing from my two co-workers. Their voices overpower the subtle sounds of the metal spatula scraping the old "fry bake" pan. These sounds were muddled by the hiss of the camp stove. The aroma of fresh coffee permeates the air. The familiar smell of white gas and the tiny roar of the WhisperLite stove comforts me as I begin to wake for the day. Fresh, crisp mountain air fills my lungs. The moist, earthy smell of the trees and dirt fill me with hope, wonder, and awe. Being wrapped in a cocoon of warmth overnight in my snug mummy sleeping bag, I had slept deep, and the residual feelings of my dreams still lingered. Peeking my head out from under the hood of my sleeping bag, I look around. My eyes meet golden sunlight. My cheeks cool from the morning high alpine air. My stomach fills with butterflies...This is living the dream!

The soft breeze bounces the tiny alpine plants. Grabbing my attention it snaps my swirling thoughts into the full present moment of the day. My senses sharpen and focus. I absorb the tiniest of details, drinking in the moment offered. The warmth radiates from the earth as the sun moves higher in the sky and the air currents begin to shift. The sunlight illuminates the scattered dew drops that magnify sparse tiny green leaves. My breath escapes me and I am filled with the sweet smells of this wild place. I feel alive, eager to move and explore, but also happy to lay belly to belly with the earth and drink in the moment. My being absorbs this as deep nourishment for my soul.

This is what I live for: to sleep on the earth wrapped snug in its elements. To breathe the dirt, to eat the sand, to wear sticks and dried leaves woven in my hair. I live for the freedom to carry only what I need on my back, plus a few hitchhikers that attach for the ride with the hope of scattering their seeds in new locations. To enjoy the beauty of the day, no matter the weather or location. Yes, this is what I live for.

Each transition is unique and ever-changing out here in the Wilderness. Each night I nestle and fall asleep on a new patch of earth that becomes my home for a brief moment in time. Each morning I am greeted by the earth in a new way, the sun lighting up the unique landscapes around me. Each day I set out on a journey with a tentative destination. Getting out the pencil, the "X" is drawn on the map as a possible camp for the evening. That location is a reasonable distance away and has potential for drinking water and a flat piece of earth to sleep on. That's all I need.

The image of the terrain ahead is created in my mind by the contour lines depicted on the tattered topographical map. This gives a glimpse of what the travel of the day ahead might hold but nowhere near a full picture.

I slide out of my sleeping bag, exposing my body and long un-derwear to the cool mountain air. Standing barefoot, the warmth gathered from my night's sleep dissipates. I stretch, yawn, and turn to look in all directions. The feeling of expansiveness hits me, giving me chills. In the distance I can hear the other instructor, Mark, belting out his favorite morning tune. "One more cup of coffee before I go." I knew I had the best job in the world.

Now ready to begin the day, I make my way toward our backcountry "kitchen." Lifting my bare feet quickly over the sharp rocks to minimize the pain, I carry my old worn black sneakers tucked under my arm. This is day 21 on a 30-day backcountry expedition: my first course as an instructor for the National Outdoor Leadership School, or NOLS.

Soon the three of us instructors gather around the stove, waiting for the water to bubble. "It's fish eyes!" Mark calls out excitedly. I could see there were small bubbles rising from the bottom of the silver-colored pot. The bubbles resemble fish eyes, so that means the water is hot enough to be considered "safe" for drinking. "Time for coffee round two!" Mark yells as we grab our travel French press mugs.

Today was the day that our students would travel without us, without the instructors. We had been preparing them over the past few weeks, teaching wilderness, first aid, and group skills. I was feeling excited for them and also a bit nervous. I mean, what if I had failed in teaching? Sipping coffee from my mug I turn to the other instructors, "What if they don't show up to the destination?" or "What if they miss the "X" on the map?" The Course Leader, a sweet and very experienced woman from Kenya, soothes my nerves with her reassurance. The Course Leader had led countless backpacking expeditions and was very aware of the students' progress. We all had worked diligently and had assessed and discussed each student's skills. My worries soon turn to excitement and then quickly to celebration.

Standing on top of a mountain in the Wind River range in Wyoming that August of 2006, we celebrated. Tilting my well-loved travel mug, I poured a little offering of coffee on the earth. This was to honor all of our "friends back home working in their cubicles." We were fortunate to be out in the wild, while many of our friends had taken office jobs. Coffee was something my instructor team thoroughly enjoyed in the backcountry. The flavor, the process, the smell, it was all a ritual unique to each connoisseur. Each instructor had their own method of storing, preparing, and consuming their coffee. We rationed just enough to make it through the expedition. Every bit of weight counts when you carry it hundreds of miles on your back up and down mountains, canyons, and off trail. So, offering one of our favorite and most cherished rituals seemed appropriate. The dry earth accepted the offering, absorbing the freshly poured coffee.

For me this was a celebration of a long thread of hard work and dedication to my path. I celebrated because I was actually living my dream. I was celebrating how far I had come. To be working for the National Outdoor Leadership School, in my mind, was the greatest accomplishment of my life. There was nothing greater in my imagination that I could have experienced. It took me 10 years to get to that moment—to view that exact view! I mean, I was standing on a mountain in a range of majestic mountain peaks, snow, and glaciers. I overlooked the expanding wilderness, "How amazing is this?" I felt I had found my life's work.

The path I took to that moment involved dedicating 10 years of my life to college and deepening my study and practice of the outdoors. I learned and refined my wilderness skills, dove into technical rock climbing and backpacking. I obsessed over canoeing, caving, survival, wilderness medicine, leadership, and teaching skills. I sat in college classrooms next to the only sliver of a window in the back corner, desperate for sunlight awaiting the day to lead groups outdoors. I viewed transparencies on the overhead projector with the monotonous yet important explanations of risk management, learning standards, and environmental problems. All while craving the outdoors and real connections with people and nature on wilderness adventures.

It was in navigating the peaks of the Wind River range where I finally felt that I had reached the summit of my dreams: to be in the high mountains guiding people who really enjoyed being out in the backcountry. I could look out for miles and it was wilderness in all directions. I felt a freedom and a comfort being out there. And each day there was a new adventure and an amazing expression of Earth and her inhabitants to see. I felt expansive and more alive than I had ever felt before in my life.

After the 30-day expedition was complete and the students left for home, we unpacked, cleaned, and finished debriefs and paperwork. We sat over breakfast and talked about what went well and what we could do better next time. I received feedback from my Instructor Team and from there I thought about my next steps in my life and career. What do you do when you have reached the summit of a dream? You look at the next peak.

18. The Crossroads

Pulling up to the stop sign I found myself at a crossroads, literally. I looked to the west and saw the Grand Teton Mountains. "I could climb those tomorrow," I thought, knowing my friends were already planning the trip. Then I turned and looked toward the east. I imagined seeing the Atlantic Ocean off the coast of Maine, the sparkles of light dancing from the water's surface. I felt it and I knew it was time to return home to see my family.

I decided to drive straight home to Maine, only stopping once to sleep at a travel plaza in New York. It was a long trip by myself, but I knew it was necessary for me. The days on the road and living in my car and out of a backpack were fun but also lonely.

It wasn't long before I found myself back in Maine to the surprise of my family. After the initial excitement of being home wore off, I knew I had to find a job. Sitting at my sister's computer, I watched as each line of my cover letters and outdoor resumes printed. I packaged them, ready to send off to potential outdoor-based schools in the area. There were several that looked promising.

My goal was to work for a school during the academic year and then return to wilderness guiding out West the following summer and then eventually become a full-time wilderness instructor. I dreamed of big adventures, glacier travel, and wilderness. I dreamed of helping others gain the confidence and skills they needed to be leaders and guides in their communities and the outdoors.

One high school I applied to had two campuses, one was located in Maine while the other was out of state. My desire was to stay in Maine close to my family. The Head of Wilderness Faculty from the school called my cell phone. After a brief conversation he shared, "We would like to offer you the job." "That's great!" I said with an exaggerated exhale. "You would live on the Connecticut campus."

The word "great" came out of my mouth, again, but I felt uneasy. I would have to travel back and forth from Connecticut to Maine. I was excited for the opportunity to design an outdoor program for the school and that is the only reason why I accepted the job in that location, and I thought the drive wouldn't be too far considering I was not all the way out West again. So I settled for the best option I could find in that moment.

I packed my Mazda Tribute with a few things and headed down to begin work at the high school. I had to go clothes shopping because there was a dress code and I owned nothing that would be suitable! How funny I felt in dress shoes and pants and button shirts walking on campus. This was a big change from cargo pants, day hikers, and a hooded sweatshirt. It didn't really feel like me, but there I was, dressed in my best Patagonia and ready to take on the world.

While planning activities for the new outdoor program, the faculty had found a project relatively close to the school. It involved cleaning up a local campground. It was fall and the owners wanted this to be completed before the campers arrived the following summer.

I drove my silver Mazda behind the school bus each day to the campground. Sometimes former students or interns would come and help me with lunch. I soon realized that the students I was working with were ones that were sent there. The numbers grew until I was responsible for 13 students, all of whom didn't want to be there.

There was a small lake at the campground and with fall approaching, the leaves were starting to turn so the colors were vibrant and beautiful. The colors reflected off the water of the lake. But we didn't have much time to sit and observe, we had a lot of work to do. Most of the clean up happened during day trips. However one weekend we camped out in the big, green Eureka tents with a handful of the students. Cooking was done with everyone's help directly on the fire. I shared stories with the students as we gathered around the crackling campfire. It was nice to share these moments with the students. They weren't aware we would be waking up with a cold swim in the morning, so we didn't ruin the moment and let them know until the sun was rising.

After raking leaves and removing brush for that one weekend at the camp, I returned to my apartment on campus late on Sunday evening. I woke up during the night not feeling very well. The following day was Monday and luckily it was my day off. I was sweating and feeling nauseous.

Dizziness took over so I dragged one of the mattresses from the bedroom down onto the floor of my living room. I pulled out a DVD I had received in the mail from my younger sister who had copied and sent it to me. I popped it into the old DVD player.

I couldn't sit up very long, the room felt like it was spinning, and the gravity felt so strong so I lay close to the floor.

At one point the DVD kept playing over and over. It was playing the same "super size me" song from that McDonald's movie. I went in and out of sleep all day, with a high fever. The repetitive sound of the song was exhausting and I wanted to throw up, but I couldn't move. I couldn't even crawl to the DVD player to turn off the movie.

The following morning I woke up and felt a little better so I turned off the DVD player and TV and walked across campus to my new office. This was so cool, my first office! The staff were locating a computer for me, and I hung my NOLS calendar on the wall with a tack. I never really imagined myself having an office, but here I was, feeling all official in my Patagonia pants and shirt, dress shoes, and an office desk.

I was still a little woozy, and breaking out in frequent sweats which was unusual. My headache was still holding on strong as well. Feeling nauseous, I told my coworkers I thought I had the flu and needed to go home and rest. I made my way back across campus, pretty exhausted and went back into my upstairs apartment. I collapsed on my bed and fell asleep for the rest of the night. This seemed to continue, periods of nausea, headaches, and exhaustion. I used to be so athletic and climb mountains and now I was struggling to get up the stairs to my second floor apartment.

19. Confusion & the Pressure to Give 110%

I kept moving along trying to learn the ins and outs of having a new job and being part of a new school community while also noticing health issues. Gradually I was learning, until one day things seemed very different. I began to feel very confused as I clenched with frustration. I am usually such a quick learner, and able to adapt and apply what I've learned to new situations. But on this beautiful fall day in September of 2006, I was having trouble planning a simple three-day outing.

I sat on the carpeted floor of my new apartment, several maps open in front of me. Just a few months ago I had planned and co-led a 30-day expedition into the Wilderness of Wyoming. But now I struggled. My eyes bounced around the map unable to stay focused. As I tried to count the elevation lines of the hikes, I'd lose count and would have to count again over and over. I couldn't seem to add simple elevations and found it frustrating trying to do the math to estimate how long it would take us for the hike.

I was nauseous, sweaty and strangely uncomfortable. My head buzzed and I felt distant from this work that used to come so easily. I tried to calculate and plan several trip options, but my mind wandered and not being able to remember the numbers, I decided to rest for a while. Folding up the maps became another puzzle and I just tossed them aside with my notes for another day when I would be able to think more clearly.

I lay on my couch. It was just big enough for two people sitting, so my legs dangled over the arm of the couch on one end and my head rested snug in the opposite corner. The room seemed to spin around me and the day passed by without me knowing. "Where did the time go?"

Nighttime became very frightening. Sleeping was a challenge and on top of that, waking with nightmares every few minutes was terrifying. This became the pattern. Being exhausted, falling asleep late, and waking up drenched in sweat every hour of the night, with my heart beating so hard in my chest. Forgetting about this once I started my day, I struggled. I began to have a hard time remembering my work schedule. I'd arrive at the school and the other faculty would ask, "Why are you in the office on your day off?" I would try to respond normally. "Oh, I just needed to hang up this calendar, that's all." I pretended that I was fine and continued on. But the scary thing was that I was unaware that it was my day off.

We were preparing for the annual family canoe and camping weekend. We needed to have split wood ready for the fire and yet that day I could barely lift the axe. Bringing the axe down it would bounce off the wood and I would have to stop and catch my breath. Seeing me struggle, one of the other instructors picked up an axe to help. I tried to make light of the situation, laughing and joking. But this was very unlike me. "What is wrong with me?" I felt a strange, full feeling as if my belly was full of bubbles, and my muscles were so fatigued. I was exhausted; I just wanted to lay down and nap. I shook and trembled with chills and my arms and hands would twitch and tremble uncontrollably. The night sweats, nightmares, insomnia, and anxiety kept me awake and in a vicious cycle.

A mother of one of the students said to me when I couldn't quite explain where we were in relation to Bath, Maine, "And you are going to be guiding us?" I grew up in this same area of Maine, and I had studied extensively. I was an instructor for one of the greatest outdoor leadership schools in the world, and I was struggling to not only communicate with these parents, but to just make it through the day as a normal person.

I snuck into my tent, crawled inside my mummy sleeping bag, and lay on my back letting out a sigh. The sound of the zipper passing my ear comforted me for a short moment as I sunk deeply into my sleeping bag. A safe, quiet, cozy place. Or so it used to be. I wore every bit of clothing to cover my body, and several hats on my head. I dreaded going back out to the fire to share stories which was the next task on the agenda. I felt sad, scared, and wanted so desperately to get a good night's sleep.

Before the debrief, I wanted to just head straight home. But it was protocol to debrief the weekend before anyone left. I said, "I'm tired and I don't feel well." "I'm tired of hearing you say I'm sick and tired, everyday," said the Director of the Wilderness Faculty. "Hmmmm?" I thought. "What was he talking about?"

He told me I would need to talk with the Head of the School to decide if I really wanted to keep working there. His assumption, or what he told me was that I was depressed. "You have the classic symptoms," he said. I left the debrief and the weekend feeling even more confused. I was left trying to figure out what

I was depressed about. It ran through my mind for the entire five-hour drive back downstate.

Back in my apartment on the Connecticut campus the following day the phone rang. "Jaclyn are you coming in? You have a classroom of 13 students waiting for you." "Oh shoot, it's Wednesday?" Somehow the schedule and the days of the week kept slipping my mind. What was wrong with me, why couldn't I figure out this schedule?

I became more and more forgetful, and more and more exhausted each day. The trouble was that I wouldn't feel well, but I would forget that I didn't feel well. I know it's bizarre, but that is how it was. It always seemed like a new thing to me, although it had been going on for three weeks already.

Again I was encouraged to go to the Head of School, but this time it was to discuss my attitude and inability to put forth 110% In talking with her, she said that I did sound depressed and that I should take two weeks off to decide if I could come back and give 110%.

So that day I left and drove toward my parent's home in Maine to rest and gain clarity, and to think about how I had been acting. Once back home, I became even more tired. I had never been so exhausted or confused in my entire life. I slept, and then visited the ocean seeking direction. While lost in the coastal mist, I decided there was no way that I could go back to work feeling like this, and I definitely couldn't give the 110% they were asking.

I struggled to walk up the hill back to the parking lot. Still breathing heavy and trying to catch my breath, I flipped open my cell phone and called the school to explain. The head of the school said, "I thought you'd be able to get back on your horse and ride again." And then she asked me to resign. I felt sad— never had I been asked to resign from a job before. But in a way, I also felt relieved. I drove home (my parents' house) walked through the door, crawled up the stairs and collapsed in my old bedroom. I lay on the floor in my sleeping bag and tried to sleep, still waking consistently with night terrors, sweats, and my heart beating out of my chest.

20. Death or Dream?

Opening my eyes, I looked around and realized I was on the floor of my old bedroom at my parents' house. I had built a nest on the floor with my sleeping bags and blankets. The remnants of last night's dreams still rolled through my mind. Recalling that last dream still so fresh in my mind, I was frightened. In the dream I was in a car accident in my silver Mazda Tribute on the entrance to the I-295 in Yarmouth, Maine. In the dream I had died and was a spirit out of my body, watching the scene as they cleaned up the five cars that were involved. There was no one else injured in that accident in that dream.

When I really came to, and remembered what day it was, I realized that this day I would go back to the school where I had been working to finalize my resignation and to move out of my apartment. Since the housing was part of the contract, I had to leave as soon as I resigned. I left my parents house feeling a little dazed and not quite with it, maybe the residual feeling from that dream had made me a little woozy. Although I didn't feel quite right, the relief of not working at that job anymore was palpable.

Once on the highway, I realized that I didn't have my apartment key with me and I would have to turn around and go back. I was about 15 minutes up the road in Portland when I began thinking about turning around. Somehow I got confused and drove in circles, not recognizing any streets before finally merging onto I-295 northbound. I made it back to my parent's house, grabbed my keys, hung the lanyard around my neck and headed off again on the southbound highway.

This day felt strange, I felt strange. It kept occuring to me that my body felt different: it was more sensitive. There was feeling like an electrical current pulsing through my nerves. I had to pay extra attention to driving because there seemed to be a lot more traffic on the highway than usual. The cars were driving fast and there were so many. I didn't remember it being this busy here in Maine, but I had been away for a while living out West so things may have changed.

As I was driving, I began to see wisps of movement that seemed to be flying around me. It was as if they were circling me while moving closer and closer. How could I concentrate on driving with all of this movement? "There are definitely more spirits here on the East Coast than there were out West," I thought confidently to myself.

It was Friday the 13th and it was October, so I concluded that the veils between worlds must be much thinner this time of year. "That's all that is going on here." I kept convincing myself as I continued driving south.

Once back on campus and in my apartment, I packed my few belongings and cleaned everything really well. I reached out to my co-workers to let them know that I was there, yet heard no response. I texted, called, and left messages. But no one returned my messages. It felt like I was in a strange place. There was absolutely no one on campus as I walked across the street to the mailroom. I checked my mailbox and then loaded my belongings into the back of my car. The seats were still folded down in the back. That's how they always were. This was the car I lived in while I was out West.

Before leaving, I thought I would do one more thing. My situation felt strange and off course, so I decided to take the time to consult the I ching. I tossed a few pennies and wrote down the heads and tails that I received. Then using a thick book, I translated what it was supposed to mean. The hexagram that I drew was called Duration. I flipped through the book, passing the dog-eared pages to the explanation about duration. It read as though I would be doing something for a long time, but I didn't have a sense of what that was. I pondered what that meant, then wrote down some quick thoughts before jumping back on the highway headed north again. As I drove further away, I felt a growing sadness for leaving a job I didn't finish. But I knew it was the right decision at the time.

My drive was about three hours long. During the drive I had time to think about so many things. My body buzzed and my thoughts were consumed with the curiosity of the spirits circling me and the dream that I had the night before. My body actually felt lifeless and the more I thought about it, the more I couldn't tell if I was actually alive or not.

As I drove by the entrance to I-295 North in Yarmouth, there was a car pile-up there on the side of the road. There were five cars, and one that was exactly like my silver Mazda Tribute. I gasped. Now I wondered if I had actually died in a car accident and I was just a lost spirit roaming the earth. I was heading to my parents' home for my sister's birthday get-together. I decided that the only way that I would know if I were alive or not, would be if I went in the house and everyone saw me then I would know I was alive. And if I went in and only my older sister Lisa could see me, then I would be just a spirit.

Turning to look over my shoulder, I gazed behind me into the back seat. I had my car packed with the seats folded down to fit all of these objects that I carried around with me. Was it that important to drive three hours to pick up these things? What if I were just a spirit and I was stuck in this world because I couldn't give up my belongings? I couldn't unattach myself from these things? Who would I be without all of this stuff?

More quickly than I realized, I turned into my parents' driveway. I parked my car and went inside. Everything seemed normal, so after the party, I slipped upstairs to my sleeping bag on the floor, slid in, zipped myself up, and settled in for the duration of the night. I was cozy for the first few minutes, but soon the night terrors and sweating forced me awake. With a click of the switch, I turned on the small lamp beside me and waited for the sun to rise.

21. The Crow In My Closet

I lay in the cozy nest on the floor of my parents' home in my old bedroom beneath that old familiar skylight. "Maybe if I could just get some rest, I will feel better," I thought. In my mind I would turn over the scenario that if anyone asks what has been going on I will tell them, "I feel nauseous, it feels like I have bubbles in my stomach and my head doesn't feel right. I keep seeing images like flashcards passing quickly in my mind." That is the only way I could think to explain what was going on. It was a bizarre feeling, but it would go away and I would feel okay for a little while. I didn't want to tell anyone because I thought they would think I was crazy but at the same time, I did feel like something was really wrong.

I awoke one morning to the sound of crows pecking at the roof of the house. Their eerie calls seemed to echo through the neighborhood. The air was cool, another damp fall day in Maine. The wind blew the leaves that had fallen from the trees. Just from the caws, I imagined there were hundreds of crows outside my window, a murder of crows. I could hear their claws scratching the roof as they bounced and walked across the shingles. Then they began to peck at the skylight directly above me. I could see their black lustrous feathers clearly through the glass, their black beady eyes staring right through me. And then I witnessed one of the crows fly through the closed skylight and I watched as the black shadow flew straight into my closet. "That was bizarre," I thought. "What unusual behaviour for a crow." I didn't want this bird flying around my bedroom, so I got myself up and closed the closet door making sure the crow wouldn't escape.

I lay back down and went to sleep. When I woke again, I could still hear that crow in my closet. Not wanting to freak my mother out, I called my older sister Lisa to explain what I had just seen. She thought it must have been a spirit crow so we tried to figure out what that could mean drawing spiritual messages from this bizarre experience. Maybe it was a messenger, maybe it meant that magic really existed. Whatever it was, it felt good to me to know that there was a reason for the crow in my closet.

22. The Dreaded Diagnosis

"**M**aybe if I take a shower, I will feel better," I thought. In my parents' bathroom, I turned on the faucet in the bathtub and tested the warmth of the water with my hand. It was warm and the steam started to fill the bathroom. As I turned to get in the shower, something in the mirror caught my eye. So I paused, then backed up to take a closer look at the reflection of my back in the mirror.

I could see a familiar expanding red rash slightly raised, with clearing in the center. I was shocked. Everything from the past few weeks came flooding into my mind and suddenly it all made sense. I knew immediately what this was. The flu-like symptoms, headaches, forgetfulness, the rash. This was no doubt Lyme disease.

I showed my parents immediately. In a way, I was happy to finally know what it was. I thought, "Great, now I can be treated and get back on with my life." And that day I began an antibiotic prescribed by my physician. I had been diagnosed with Lyme disease because of the obvious bull's-eye rash and flu-like symptoms I had been experiencing. Blood tests were taken and sent off to the lab.

By the time of this diagnosis, I was already thinking, "If I die I don't want people to see this mess I've created in my life. I don't want anyone to see how I lived." My mind was not functioning correctly and I was immersed in paranoia. I couldn't tell what was real and what wasn't. I had begun to prepare for my death, without anyone else knowing.

Lyme is caused by the bite of a tick that transfers a spirochete, a spiral shaped bacterium, into the body. The bite is often not felt because the ticks have a numbing agent in their saliva and the ticks are very tiny. I never saw the tick, but I felt the effects pretty immediately.

My rash was big, larger than the size of my hand. It was on my back so I hadn't seen it. I didn't feel it either! The rash was not itchy or sore. Still, how could an illness be this severe and affect my thoughts and body to such a degree, yet go rather unnoticed for three weeks?

Nevertheless, I was relieved to have a name for this illness and to have my family aware, somewhat, of what was going on. Given my treatment, a 14-day course of antibiotics, I should expect to get better and would be able to return to work within a few weeks. I called the school where I had been working when I fell ill. If I had contracted Lyme disease while working there, it would be likely that the students may have been exposed as well. I called out of concern for those students, yet I was met with a response I didn't expect. The school quickly cancelled all of my health insurance benefits and filed a worker's compensation claim which wasn't my intent. Further I was not allowed back at the school or to talk with anyone, and their lawyer contacted me. It was a very scary and stressful time. I decided that when I did get better (in two weeks) I will look for another job as this one didn't seem to respect me or my skills.

23. Early Diagnosis and the ER

I didn't know what being an athlete meant to me until I found myself gasping for air with what felt like my heart pounding out of my chest. Just climbing a simple set of stairs in my home was a monumental task. Just a few weeks before, I was on top of majestic mountain peaks, living it up as an adventurous Wilderness Guide in the high mountains of Wyoming while exploring new lands by myself. I traveled thousands of miles alone, living out of my small SUV and cooking on my backpacking stove. It was just me and the road, rivers, mountains, caves, and deserts. I felt empowered and filled to the brim with living an adventurous life. I was living a life of my deepest dreams and desires. So how is it possible for all of this to change so drastically, and so quickly?

All of a sudden I found myself living minute to minute. Each move forward was just getting to the next breath. The forgetfulness was sort of a savior; luckily it wouldn't let me remember the excruciating pain or panic for very long.

I was a wilderness guide and so of course I had heard about Lyme and that typical bull's-eye rash that is a telltale sign of an infection with borrelia burgdorferi (bb). But what I learned was that it was hard to catch and easy to cure. So I embraced the

14-day course of antibiotics with the expectation that I'd be back to work in a few short weeks.

"Wonderful, I can handle this. Some quick down time and rest and I'll be back in the wilderness in no time," I thought, happy to finally know what was wrong and to have a clear path forward. But what little did I actually know!

When I began to take antibiotics, everything intensified, everything got worse. My nerves burned and the pressure inside my skull felt like my head was going to burst completely open. It felt like my skull was in a vice that was constantly being squeezed tighter and tighter. The light caused excruciating pain in my eyes and every little sound was amplified. The ticking of the clock, the drip of a leaky faucet, the furnace and the hot air blowing the curtains echoed loudly through my mind. Everything sounded like fingernails on a blackboard. I rolled on the floor writhing in pain that I thought would never stop. I didn't think I'd be able to handle it, it felt like I was being torn open from the inside.

My mother was so concerned that she immediately called my doctor and I was admitted to the ER under his advice to rule out EEE (Eastern Equine Encephalitis) which was the current scare in the vector-borne illness world. The threat of mosquitoes transmitting EEE was all over the news at the time.

Yes, I was paranoid. Yes, I was in severe pain from head to toe. The rash had disappeared though, and so with it the visual evidence that I had Lyme disease. My medical records showed the recent diagnosis based on the obvious rash and symptoms, however since it was so soon after finding the rash, the blood tests weren't back yet.

The doctors laughed a bit and looked at where the rash was, scraping the little bit of dry skin. At the time I saw the rash, it was at least eight inches across and expanding, but a few days later it was just a dry, flaky, patch of skin.

"So why are these ER docs so suspicious?" I thought. They didn't believe that I had Lyme, or that any of the psychosis symptoms were related. I don't know how to explain how I felt, or how we were treated at the ER that night. All I can say is that I was terrified and the doctors' responses intensified my uneasiness. Instead of feeling better, I felt scrutinized.

I was sent to a small bathroom to take a urine sample. I had a very hard time following the instructions, the "simple" step-by-step process written in tiny words were a blur. It didn't make sense. But I managed and when I came out of the bathroom, I immediately began to panic. Everything inside me was shaking. I couldn't remember where I had come from. I felt dizzy and nauseous. I felt a hot flash and my entire body felt like it was burning. I decided to keep calm and take this one step at a time.

Walking slowly forward I wondered why it was so hard to lift my legs and move? I was thinking to myself, "I will remember something soon, just keep moving. Don't look suspicious. Don't look like you don't know what's going on."

The movement, the groans from other patients, the smell of the hospital, the crinkle of plastic, and the chaos in the ER added to my panicked state that I was trying so desperately to keep inside. I didn't trust these people here, these nurses or doctors. The lights and noise were so confusing I couldn't think, and then I saw the familiar face of my mom sitting in the chair next to the bed and I felt like everything was going to be alright.

My mother and I were then guided to another part of the hospital, and I thought they must have found a cure for me! But the two people we met asked me to change my clothes. They asked if I had anything sharp, any weapons, or any drugs. I took everything out of my pockets, my hair ties, pocket change, Chapstick, and they handed me hospital clothes. Then they proceeded to inventory and lock up all of my belongings. Turning a key in the closed door until it clicked, they pushed the door to a room open revealing people in obvious distress. The nurses guided me into another closed room with a bed I could lay on and a chair for my mom to sit. I lay down to rest, trying to block out the lights and the sound. The nurses drew my blood every hour. The quick CT scan showed nothing of significance and there were no drugs in my system.

A gentleman came in and sat cross-legged in front of me with a clipboard full of papers and began to ask a series of questions. He held his pencil up, playing with it as he went down the list, the pencil scratching on the paper as he scribbled notes from our discussion.

Part of me thought these questions to be very strange and unlike what a medical doctor should be asking. I had to concentrate really hard to hear him, and to understand what he was asking. It was so hard to communicate; my brain was working so slowly and it was hard to recall information from earlier in my life. Part of me told me not to tell him everything, and so I didn't.

I was afraid to tell him that I had been hearing voices and I could hear what sounded like a scanning of dozens of radio stations with static overlaying all of them. My vision was different. I saw colors, I smelled things that weren't there such as apple pies baking and could hear common cell phone rings that obviously weren't really there. After he completed this line of questioning, he left for quite some time and then returned.

"You have an unusual late onset of paranoid schizophrenia or possibly bipolar disorder," he said in a matter-of-fact manner. "Here is a pamphlet on mental health disorders, and here is a pamphlet on schizophrenia and one on bipolar that you can read through with your mom to familiarize yourself. You are welcome to go home now and then follow up with your primary care physician for further diagnosis and treatment."

My thoughts went immediately to, "So now I have Lyme disease and schizophrenia?" My life felt like it had fallen apart in just a few short weeks. How could I go from such a free and adventurous lifestyle to this nightmare? I was completely and most undoubtedly devastated.

So, I went home to rest, the headache subsided, and I curled up in my nest on the floor of the bedroom while my mom made an appointment with my primary care doctor. He has known me my whole life, and my family for a long time. I was confident that at least he would be able to help.

We arrived and walked through the door to the office of my primary care doctor. The smiling face of the nurse behind the desk calmed my nerves. She was always so kind and gentle in her words as she guided us to the room, catching up with my mom and checking in with me as she took my blood pressure and weight. Then left us to settle before the doctor came in.

I listened to the music that was playing faintly in the background while laying on my back. Gazing at the ceiling tiles, I realized how exhausted I felt. This experience was tearing me apart inside. I was startled by the knock on the door, and then in walked the doctor. He was always ready to listen no matter how long it took. He gathered as much information as possible to best be able to problem-solve the situation.

After a few minutes speaking about the recent events, we tossed the mental health pamphlets out with that diagnosis and continued the antibiotics for 30 days. There were improvements with my symptoms over the past few weeks and my condition really had started to turn around. We thought the two extra weeks would resolve everything. I returned to the doctor's office at that time, and the antibiotic treatment was stopped at that point. I was feeling really good and had no symptoms for about a week or so and I was expected to fully recover and be back to work. What a journey this was!

24. "Post-Lyme Syndrome" A True Quest For Healing

J ust two days after stopping the antibiotics, my symptoms returned. The buzzing in my body, fatigue, and the fever all came back. I was quickly referred to an infectious disease specialist who quickly diagnosed me with "post-Lyme syndrome."

The doctor assured me in a confident manner that my body had fought the Lyme bacteria and defeated it. He explained that my immune system was "stuck on" and was attacking my own body. He assured me that this happens on occasion and usually resolves in a few weeks. Well that was good news to me. I still had in my mind the dream of returning back to the wilderness and back to work.

He went on to explain that I should begin to see improvements without any further treatment. My body would surely return to balance, I would just need to be patient. But a few weeks later at my follow-up appointment with the infectious disease specialist, my symptoms had grown much worse.

Since the Lyme was cured (phew!) I was tested for what seemed to be every known illness under the sun. The uncertainty left me feeling more afraid everyday. Being in the complete unknown as

I awaited test results after test results left me struggling. I was tested for diabetes and then hepatitis and syphilis. When those were negative, I had to fill out anonymous paperwork for HIV testing. As every test was sent away for evaluation, I was left scared awaiting the results—although I thought knowing what I had would bring peace to my mind. I knew I wasn't well. But test after test returned and there was no new information. So my continued diagnosis was "post-Lyme syndrome."

With no answers, I continued searching for the next two-and-a-half years for the cause of this elusive illness. The post-Lyme syndrome was even worse than the original Lyme disease. There were times when I was afraid that I would die in my sleep, and times when I felt so awful that I wished I would. To be so sick on the inside and so confused, while doctors told me, "It's all in your head" or "We've done all we can do, you are just going to have to learn to live like this," I began to lose hope. I lost the hope of ever knowing, or ever getting better.

With hundreds of hours in waiting rooms and many miles traveled, my condition continued to worsen as I added to my arsenal of diagnoses. A handful I gathered were: post-Lyme syndrome, myofascial pain disorder, chronic fatigue syndrome, fibromyalgia, visual midline shift syndrome, post trauma vision syndrome, depression, anxiety disorder, attention deficit disorder, gastroparesis, and gastritis to name a few.

But none of these got to the root of what was causing all of this and treating these symptoms separately backfired many times, forcing me deeper into confusion and illness. I studied online and in the Lyme chat groups, but the discussions there were far from hopeful and I felt myself growing more sick and angry every day.

25. Seeking Help Out of State

After visiting many doctors in Maine, my primary doctor sent me out of state to a specialist at a teaching hospital in Connecticut. Lyme disease first emerged in Lyme, Connecticut in the 1970s and so this new avenue gave me hope. "They must have so much experience, they will be able to help me," I thought to myself awaiting the day in the future when we would finally get in for an appointment.

My mom, aunt, and I packed a few snacks and piled in the car for the long drive to Connecticut. I was going to see another infectious disease specialist, whom I was sure had seen many cases of Lyme disease.

We sat in the exam room waiting as he flipped through my thick chart. By this time I was about two years into my health crisis and my medical files were pretty extensive. But it seemed to me, since I had Lyme disease that never got better, my issues now were most likely related somehow.

The doctor peered down through his glasses as he flipped slowly through the papers, looking up slightly every few seconds to ask a few questions. When he reached the bottom of the pile he turned and looked at me and told me the best advice he had for me that day. "Do you have a YMCA near you?" "Yes,"

I replied, trying to sit up straight with confidence despite the sharp pains running through my body and intense fatigue. "Then you should join an exercise group so you will be more motivated to get your ass out of bed."

At first I couldn't believe what I was hearing. I was completely shocked at this advice coming from the doctor's mouth. "When in a group, people tend to be more motivated." My mom was taken aback by these words as well. We had driven so far to see who we thought would be the best Lyme specialist in New England.

This response sent my mind into a whirlwind. All of the words I had been hearing over the past few years from doctors and professionals swirled through my head. I heard echoing in my mind, "We have done all we can do, you are going to have to just learn to live like this."

I was told that I was depressed, that I needed to push myself to exercise. Some said that I looked like a healthy young woman. People around me advised me to stop complaining, and to just get over it. Doctors told me it was all in my head.

But for me it was real. I felt awful every day. It was like having a brain injury and the flu every day for two straight years without a break.

When the tests don't show anything positive, do we just ignore the person's symptoms and degrading health? What was happening inside me felt so wrong. I felt so ill, this wasn't me. I so desperately wanted to be well again.

My free spirit missed the mountains, the fresh air, and the views from those high peaks. I missed traveling. I missed adventures and freedom. Why would they say I am making this up? And seeing this doctor, at this moment, I wanted to just give up. To give in. After this two-year battle I wanted to "throw in the towel."

26. Invisible Illness

There was a constant deep buzz pulsing through my nervous system. My arms and legs began to twitch erratically. Losing control of my body to this extent led me to believe that I would never be able to get any better. No one knew what was wrong with me and worse, no one could help. Every day I felt very close to death, as if it were breathing down my neck. I lived in constant fear, anxiety, and disappointment. The medical system and the way I was treated was devastating to my spirit.

My digestive system began to shut down and my stomach stopped functioning efficiently. I was one of the youngest people at the gastroenterologist with what they called "gastroparesis." Apparently the nerve that tells my stomach what to do was damaged, however it wasn't linked to Lyme disease at the time.

There was no reason why I had this nerve issue. The doctors said this usually occurs with people who have diabetes, and I was tested again and again the test was negative. Eating a small bite of food would leave me nauseous, and with no way to digest it, the irritation made my stomach burn and I would eventually throw up. I couldn't take this anymore, the headaches were excruciating. My whole body ached, every muscle.

It appeared my muscles were disintegrating. As my once strong and healthy body slowly disappeared, I let go of all my former dreams and aspirations. I thought that I would slowly vanish into thin air.

Some of the scariest moments were literally not knowing who I was. No matter how hard I tried, I couldn't recall my name, how old I was, or even if I were male or female. I found an old piece of newspaper from 1978, my birth announcement. The tiny square was yellowed and worn. I read the piece of paper each morning, "Jaclyn Amanda Ouillette was born to…" It gave me my birthday, my parents names, and my grandparents names. It gave me the town we lived in. I prayed to remember who I was and mumbled these words as often as I could.

There was a feeling inside of me that I knew all of this, but it just wouldn't come to me. My sisters would come to visit and through a haze I would focus on their faces. They were familiar to me, but who were they? I couldn't recall their names or remember how I knew them. I should know them, I think I do but...

At times I would be standing at a store in front of a cashier, holding dollars and change in my hand staring blankly as I had forgotten how to count money. The feeling of embarrassment would come over me as I knew these were things I should know but didn't. I couldn't seem to add, couldn't read, and couldn't hold a conversation.

To find myself lost in my parents home, where I had lived since I was four years old, made me feel like I was losing my mind. Sometimes I would wander from room to room, unable to recall what I was doing there. There must be a reason to come into this room, maybe I was getting something? Then standing in the next room, I wouldn't recognize where I was.

Even leaving the house became impossible—an insurmountable and dangerous task. Sometimes it was difficult to find my way back to the house from the mailbox. It might sound bizarre, but it was very real to me, and very scary. I was frightened.

My sister called me in the morning as she did almost every day for two and a half years. "I will come pick you up," she said. "Be ready." "Okay I will, I won't forget this time," I said. And then as soon as I hung up the phone, I would begin to get ready. Then I would hear a car pull into the driveway and I would peek out the blinds to see who was there. I didn't recognize the car. I remember thinking, "My sister has a bigger car, this couldn't be her." But then she would get out and come knock on the door. "Oh shoot," I'd realize that I was still in my pajamas. I'd let her in and then rush to get dressed, trying not to let on that I had no idea what we were doing that day.

I climbed in the car and off we went. I probably asked the same questions over and over and she kindly repeated the same answers over and over with a little smile. "Where are we going?" I would ask. Forgetting the response I would ask again, "Where are we going?"

This happened day in and day out. She took me out to get fresh air. We walked by the river down the street from my parents' home and on the small sandy beach in our hometown, and every once in a while she would take me along to run errands.

We arrived, parked in the parking lot, and walked into the store together. She grabbed a cart, picked up her daughter, set her in the front of the cart, and buckled her in. I remember her saying she was going somewhere and I would wait for her where I was.

Just after she left, I looked around and realized that I didn't know where I was. Everything was red and I couldn't make out the shapes that were in front of me. There were some tall figures; I thought at first they were people but I couldn't tell for sure. The shapes were pulsing and moving, like they were breathing, but I couldn't recognize anything.

The shapes didn't fit together and I couldn't see depth. I forgot who I was there with, or how I ended up in that place at all. My heart raced as I looked around. I felt lost. I took a small step to see if anything would change and to see if I could pick up any clues to help me figure out where I was.

Trying to use what I could see to put together the story, I noticed that almost everything was red. "It must be Valentine's Day," I concluded. But there was still so much confusion and unknown, I was overwhelmed. Desperately looking around to get my bearings I thought, "Where am I?" "What am I doing here?" "How did I get here?"

I must have looked strange because I heard my sister's voice come through the darkness, "Are you alright?" That was a relief to hear, and I just followed the familiar sound of her voice. The world appeared almost as a kaleidoscope, and slowly the shapes came back into focus and relation with each other. As my mind put things together, I realized we were in a store. The symbol on the cart came into focus, and I recognized it as a bull's-eye target. We were in the store, Target!

After that experience I avoided that store. Seeing all red, and then the focus being on the double red ring, it brought back the memories of the day I saw a similar sign on my back. That day two years before had changed my life forever. I think I may have had a post traumatic response to the logo. Since then, everytime I see a Target truck pass me on the highway, my body tenses and I remember that tick bite in 2006 that changed the course of my life forever.

27. A Speck of Light

One of the turning points came during an appointment at my neurologist's office. I had been in neurological rehabilitation to help me recover from brain damage caused from the initial Lyme infection. But my skills were declining in therapy rather than improving, which led my cognitive therapist to be suspicious. It was very unusual in their practice to see someone decline in such a way. My neuro-therapy team believed that something was continuing to cause damage so further testing from a neurologist was suggested.

The neurologist ran several more tests. I lay in noisy machines for MRIs, scans, painful spinal taps, and nerve testing yet nothing turned up conclusive. Having tried all he knew over several months' time, he entered the room and closed the door behind him, leaving it open just a crack to let the hall noise and the light in. Holding his clipboard, he bent down and spoke in a quiet voice to me, "You know Jackie, you may want to get a second opinion from another doctor. I've done all I can do here. I am aware that the infectious disease specialist you are seeing uses a set of guidelines for Lyme, but there are others out there who use another set of guidelines for testing and treatment of tick illness. I'd suggest you look up one of the other doctors and get a second opinion." He also gave me the name of the guidelines and how to find a "Lyme literate doctor."

I had in my own research recently come across this other set of guidelines. This newer set of guidelines says that Lyme is easy to get and often hard to treat. The guidelines state that with one bite from a tick, you can also contract a whole host of other co-infections. That day, with the help of my neurologist and cognitive therapist, I made a decision that would eventually save my life. That decision was to leave the infectious disease specialist who had convinced me that I had post-Lyme syndrome and that I didn't need any more treatment. I began to search for a Lyme literate doctor who could understand, have a new perspective, and who could actually help.

Navigating the medical system was scary and frustrating. In the emotional and mental state I was in, this was even more stressful. The doubt I had from seeing professionals who had no answers, filling out the hundreds of pages of paperwork, the approvals and denials from insurance companies, all contributed to making my healing path bumpy, rough, and very uncertain.

28. The Cave of Despair

One day after one of my doctor appointments in Yarmouth, I got into the driver's seat of my car. I took a breath and looked around. I felt strange, as if I had never been in this car before. Surely it was mine—I recognized the rocks and feathers—but I wasn't sure how to make the car move.

I took a deep breath trying to bring my memory back. I put the key in ignition and turned it. I could feel the car start up. Looking at the pedals on the floor, I could see there were two. Although I knew at this point that one would make the car go and one would make it stop, it had escaped my mind which was which.

I stopped and took another breath. "Maybe I should call someone," I thought. I pulled my cell phone out of my pocket and flipped it open. Staring at the tiny screen, I couldn't think of anyone to call, my mind was blank. How would I dial them on this little machine? None of the buttons made any sense to me so I slid the phone back in my pocket.

I looked at the shifter, and tried to remember what the P, R, N, D, 1, & 2 meant. I decided that I would give it a try and maybe I would remember. I slid the shifter from its position in P to R, and pressed on one of the pedals. My car was moving slowly backward. I found the brake quickly. Then I moved the shifter to N, and then finally to the D. Luckily home was less than a mile away and I pulled in the driveway safely, and quickly turned the car off. I checked and double-checked everything to make sure the car wasn't moving. Back inside the house, I crawled up the stairs to my bedroom. Relieved, I laid on my back to rest and collect myself.

What kind of illness would make my memory leave me? It was like a wave, coming and going. I kept moving forward hoping not to be embarrassed with not knowing how to perform simple tasks that I had once carried out so easily. It had become a struggle just to take care of myself, let alone drive anywhere. Sometimes in the middle of a drive, I would forget where I was going and would turn to go back home when I'd realize that I didn't know how to get home either. I'd have to pull off to the side of the road to park my car so I could wait until some sort of memory came back. But then one day, as I was driving my Tribute down Congress Street in the center of the city, I felt like I was in a daze. It was almost as if nothing was real. Seeing the stop lights illuminated red I remember thinking, "I know that's important...what does that mean?" as I continued to drive right through the first, second, and then the third red light. The beeps and honks coming from the other cars around me just made me more confused. Luckily I made it home safely.

My driver's license was "taken away" right after that incident. Between my doctor and my cognitive therapist, it was clear that I could not comprehend the rules required to drive a vehicle. On any given day do you stop to think about the focus and understanding you need to drive a big machine 70 mph down the highway? Or to drive on streets with other cars? Probably not.

After losing my license for medical reasons, my cognitive ability declined further right along with my physical ability. I could barely sit up, and struggled to walk down the halls. My body wasn't doing what I was asking it to do. I felt like I was failing in all directions. I tried to maintain the hope that the post-Lyme syndrome would let up, or that the correct diagnosis would be made. But with each doctor visit, each needle, and each test, my hope dwindled.

My muscles atrophied quickly. The weakness in my legs, neck, and back became more apparent as my muscles disintegrated. Sitting long enough to slurp some of my mother's homemade soup became a chore. Amazed at my ingenuity with the realization that I could heat water with the electric kettle which could then be added to the soup. This was an amazing discovery since I couldn't stand long enough for a pot to simmer on the stove. I had to be careful as well as I might forget the soup on the stove and have all the water boil out before I realized it (which happened on several occasions.)

The daily excruciating headaches and body aches that radiated and jumped from one part of my body to another overwhelmed me. The frequent hallucinations exhausted me. The light and sound was intensified and it was as if my brain couldn't filter out the extra noise and patterns that it used to.

Even my quiet bedroom was overwhelming with the amount of movement I saw. With exhaustion and weakness, I crawled across the floor to get from my bedroom to the bathroom (which was downstairs.) To climb the stairs I used my arms to help pull me up because I was too weak and tired to stand, let alone walk.

I'd lay at the top of the stairs to rest and catch my breath, knowing my bed was in sight. Sometimes I would fall asleep right there, my face on the rough carpet. "Build up your strength," I'd tell my body while laying there. I had to garner the strength to make it the few yards back to my bed.

I was too weak to carry a laundry basket or to even hold a cup of tea and the nightmares and night sweats continued. "How am I creating this? Why would I make this up?" These thoughts tumbled around my mind with the echoing of what the doctors and specialists had told me over the years.

These were scary times for me, when I couldn't remember my name. Who was I? Lying in my bed looking up at the textured ceiling, I'd wonder, "What year is this? What month? What season is it?" The clues and memories did not bubble up as they usually would and I felt so lost.

The light hurt my eyes, so I covered my windows with blankets to keep the sun out. I found relief in partial darkness with wax earplugs in my ears to dull the sounds. By lessening the stimulus, my nervous system could rest. Slowly I created a dark cave around me as I tried to comfort my body and spirit, yet I slipped into the deepest despair I had ever experienced.

29. The Voice

Now more than two years into being in bed, I find myself lying in a nest of blankets on the floor consumed by overwhelming and excruciating pain. Waves of electricity shot down my legs. From hips to toes the shock would jolt me, first one side then the other. Then from my elbow to my fingers. The ceaseless movement of pain and low hum radiating, pulsing, and constantly changing was overwhelming to my overworked system.

There was a crushing feeling in my head, like my skull was in vice grips slowly getting tighter and tighter. I felt like there was pressure inside of me that was constantly pushing outward, on my spine and in my neck. My head felt so full, I thought it would crack. My neck was stiff, and I had a hard time just to hold up my head.

Desperately I wanted to be taken away from this pain. My thoughts went to ways that I could escape, convincing myself I was living a life that wasn't worth living. I thought, "maybe I could quietly slip away in the night, escape my breath and the body that holds me here." I was sure that no one would notice and wouldn't miss me when I was gone.

The constant deep buzz grew stronger, as if the very core of my being was electrified. Every tiny nerve was actively firing random, nonstop mini pulses. At times it would quicken and my heart would beat so hard my chest would bounce.

My arms, legs, and fingers jumped erratically followed by a loud popping and cracking sound that would turn my vision completely white for a split second. It was as if I had hit my head really hard on the ice, but I was just laying my head on a pillow. This was constant for more than two years straight, with no signs of relief.

Finally one day, I reached my breaking point. I mumbled out loud as best as I could, "If there is something greater than me out there, please help." I said a prayer asking for help to leave this pain...I thought the only way out of the pain was to leave this body. The pain had grown so intense it swallowed my being. I surrendered, let go, and dove into my inner world so far, that it seemed I traveled out of my body. As if I were falling through space I tumbled beyond the stars, like in a dream where you are falling and wake up with a sudden jolt. But I didn't wake up.

Eventually I came to a place where everything seemed still. I had no pain, and it was as if I had no thoughts. In that experience was peace and contentment. There was a calm voice that I could hear. "Who's there?" I felt like someone was watching me, but I couldn't see who it was. There was a strong presence and a voice filled the space with a familiar vibration. The sound soothed my body. "It is your choice to be here, and it is your choice to leave."

I was taken back to my very early life, to being a baby again, and experienced the frustration of what it felt like to be learning about my body and the world again. Then while experiencing my "toddler body," I found how cumbersome and awkward it was at the same time trying to communicate what I wanted with the adults that looked down at me. "Why didn't they understand?" I thought. My body was a toddler trying to learn to walk. At that moment I thought, "No way," my situation would be much easier than to go through being born again and learning all of this all over again. I decided I wanted to live, and if I was going to live, I was going to really live!

I promised that if I were able to get better, if I healed from this illness, I would share my story with others. The promise was clear as I stated it right then and there to the voice, myself, and the universe. I made the decision and committed to getting better.

I thought with that decision, I would come back into my body healed and ready to move on, but I didn't. I came back with a heavy thud into a clumsy body. The body that was weak, trembling, twitching, and failing. The mind that was confused and overwhelmed. I returned to the pain, heaviness, and my bedroom in my parents' home. I returned to not being able to drive or take care of myself.

In that moment or alternate reality, I had experienced a spark of hope, one of inspiration. I witnessed something much bigger than myself. "How can I muster the strength to keep going?" I asked myself...and I began to feel my determination rising. A fire had begun to smolder in my very inner core, my inner light was sparked.

There was and still there is no current cure for "chronic Lyme disease." There is no agreement amongst the medical professionals that chronic Lyme even exists. So I would need to learn to navigate my way out of this darkness. I needed to navigate by my own light to reclaim my life.

The turning point for me was, in a large part, gratitude. What I needed was to change the way I was looking at this illness and disease. What was I thankful for, in this moment, with this experience? When I spoke to that voice it was as if nothing was wrong. I was in the right place, and everything was up to me and my thoughts. There was no right or wrong, good or bad. That translated to me, "Everything is just how it is. It is up to me to determine how I respond or react to my life. My life is a creation of what I have thought and put into it." So now what? How do I change my thoughts? The answer I received was to write about my gratitude to the disease and everything it had and was still giving me.

I walked down the stairs with a crumpled, tattered paper in my hands. I had written, and crossed out, many words many times. My hands trembled and it was hard to hold the pen. The spelling of simple words escaped me. But finally what I was trying to say was out and written on this piece of paper. It felt like my heart was torn, and my raw, real self was exposed. My voice wavered as I began to read this to my parents.

Dear Disease,

I am grateful for this illness.
I appreciate your persistence.
I love your willingness to not give up on me.
You have taught me to look at life through different eyes.
You have taught me to slow down.
You have taught me the importance of breath.

You have taught me the importance of nurturing always.
You have taught me to fight back, with all of my energy
everyday, every night, every moment.
You have taught me to focus my energy only on what I truly want.
You have taught me that giving up is unacceptable.
You have taught me the power of my own thoughts.
You have taught me to look deep within.
You have taught me to remember life is beautiful.
I am truly grateful for all these learnings.
I want to thank you, for most importantly,
I have learned that
every breath, every step, every thought in life is healing.

With much love and appreciation,
Jaclyn A. Ouillette

Looking at my parents, who had tears in their eyes, I knew I had touched on something that would change the direction I was headed in. After two-and-a-half years of a downward spiral I had found a spark of hope and began to follow the tiny sparks of light that I saw. These sparks of light led me step-by-step and moment-by-moment out of that darkness.

To change the way we think about something changes everything in our life. To find gratitude in such a dark place, I had to shift the way I was thinking. Instead of focusing on everything that was not working, everything I couldn't do, I had to stop the auto-pilot thoughts that had kept me in a victim stance since close to the onset of this illness. But as I explored my thoughts, I found that this pattern went back further, before this illness. This exercise changed the way I saw and experienced life. It raised my consciousness in a way. Everyday after that day, I read the poem day and night as a reminder to myself. As a reminder to my thoughts to keep focused on the light. This experience sparked a deeper passion within myself for life and for adventure. It is that passion that began to pull me forward.

30. A Spark of Hope and Healing

As my mother and I searched for clues and insights into healing, we only found two people in Maine who shared hopeful stories in their recovery from Lyme disease. It was rare to find someone with a hopeful story! I listened as deep and as hard as I could to these two people, because they had something that I really wanted. They had improvement in their health. What was it that they did differently than the others?

One woman shared how she had been a professional dancer in New York City. She had been sick for several years with Lyme disease to the point where she was in a wheelchair because she could no longer walk or stand. When I listened to her talk softly through the phone, I could hear her strength and determination in her voice yet she expressed herself so gently to me. She was cautious with her words and I was comforted by the way she understood what I was going through. At that time, she was preparing to return to New York to begin dancing again. To hear her say that, gave me so much hope. She told me, "You have to have hope if you are going to get better." Listening to her story did fill me with more hope than I had before. If she could return to dancing, I could return to the wilderness. She shared how changing her diet helped her and how she had found a Lyme literate doctor who understood and treated her as a whole person.

I immediately began making changes to my diet and waited for the response from the Lyme literate doctors I had called. I only found two in the state of Maine through suggestions from Lyme support groups and individuals my mom and I talked with. Both practices were full and no longer accepting new patients. At times it felt like I was destined to be sick forever. But we continued to seek out more people who could share any potential answers or suggestions that could help me in my healing process.

I remember laying on the hard rug on the floor of our living room while my mom spoke to one of her co-workers. Her co-worker explained how she was sick for over 10 years in the '80s with an unknown illness that left her bed-bound. Finally she found a Lyme literate doctor in Kennebunk, was tested, and was treated for several years. She shared how much her condition improved with the treatment. She recommended the husband-and-wife doctor team who helped her, since they had real life experience with tick-borne illness and they were both doctors. My mother scribbled down the names and phone number of the Lyme literate naturopathic doctor (LLND) on a scrap piece of paper. Right after our conversation, I had my mom dial the office and I left a message on their answering machine. I decided that was the last call I was going to make. If no doctors called me back, I just didn't have the strength to keep searching and being let down.

I did, however, continue researching and adjusting my diet over the next few months. I scoured the internet for as long as

I could sit and printed out articles that might offer answers. It was hard for me to read the words on the screen, so I printed what I could in large lettering and used highlighters and skills I learned in neuro rehab to help me read and understand the papers. I purchased a used book, The Yeast Connection Cookbook, which helped me tremendously. The recipes were easy to follow and there were explanations of different foods a sensitive body could react to such as molds and sugars.

One afternoon while I was resting, the phone rang. As always, every time the phone rang I was immediately filled with anxiety. The loud and sudden noise startled me. I could hear my mom answer the phone. Then she said, "Hold on, just one minute let me get her...Jaclyn!" My mom yelled up the stairway, her voice echoing and amplifying my already shaking body. "Who is it?" "She says she's from the doctor's office."

I stumbled down the stairs to meet my mom who was half way up and I reached for the phone. "Hello?" "Hello this is Angel." A sigh of relief. "Wait a minute... is this for real?" I thought. There is an Angel calling me? I better sit down and listen a bit longer. She went on to explain, "I am from the doctor's office down in Kennebunk, you called a few months ago. We apologize we have been so busy we are just getting back to you."

It had been several months since I called and left a message on the answering machine at the doctor's office. My mother had been talking to everyone she knew about Lyme disease trying to find answers.

I was shocked that I would finally be going to see a Lyme literate doctor. They seemed so elusive and hard to find. Their practices were full and I only heard of them through the whispers from doctors who really cared about my well being and through online chat forums. Many of the Lyme literate doctors weren't listed online and I read that it was because of the fear of having their licenses revoked. Chronic Lyme disease didn't exist according to the Infectious Disease Society of America, and they were against any long term treatment. The Lyme literate doctors followed the guidelines of the International Lyme and Associated Diseases Society which stated that Lyme was easy to get and hard to treat in some patients.

I made an appointment for a consultation, but it would be three months before I could get in. After speaking with the doctor and explaining my story, he and my primary care physician agreed to start me on doxycycline until my appointment with the LLND. I was afraid to take antibiotics again; the first time I did, I ended up in the emergency room. I definitely didn't want that to happen again! I prepared myself by further limiting sugar in my diet and adding more probiotic foods and a probiotic supplement. I don't know if any of this helped, but it did make me feel more in control of my health. I had already been eating a low carb, high protein diet which seemed to have some success. I didn't eat fruits, flour, or high carb veggies. I lived mostly on miso soup, chicken, kombucha, cooked greens, sprouts, kimchi, green tea, and tofu. It seemed most everything I ate either bothered my stomach or intensified my symptoms.

I began the antibiotics, knowing it would be another journey into the unknown. The doctors thought that if I had Lyme originally, which was clearly determined by the bull's-eye rash and flu-like symptoms, and it never cleared, and I tested negative for everything else, there was a good possibility I still had Lyme.

After beginning the antibiotic, I was amazed with what happened over the next two weeks. At first I felt awful for a few days, as expected. I was more tired and achy and let my body rest as my doctors suggested. But then one morning I woke up with my thoughts clear, and the pain in my muscles was dulled. The antibiotics seemed to be helping. Ironically, my digestive system started working again!

Things were going so well, that I was able to take the driver's test again to get my license back. I had to have my vision tested and evaluated as well as my ability to comprehend driving. Sitting at the computer simulator at neurological rehabilitation, I stared at the screen. I had to understand what to do at red lights and green lights. I had to recognize signs, and it was amazing how well I did. Suzy, my Cognitive Therapist was so ecstatic for me with my results. She had been working with me for over a year and a half watching as my abilities declined, and to have a significant turn around like this was not only amazing, but very hopeful for my recovery!

Then came time for the on-the-road test. The driving instructor sat in the passenger seat and Suzy in the back, both with pens and clipboards in hand. The instructor in the front had his foot near a second brake just in case. I turned the key, shifted into drive, and began driving again. The instructor guided me to drive on the highway and in parking lots and I thought I did well. I felt confident and grateful that I didn't have to parallel park! We pulled into the parking lot for the driving school and they discussed between themselves how I did. My license was returned to me and it was determined that it was safe for me to drive again! What a relief.

I felt so good with these improvements yet also so angry because this could have happened several years before. And although there were improvements, I was still very far from true health and recovery. I knew this could be a long road, but one I was willing to walk and I finally got a glimpse of the light at the end of the tunnel. There was a mountain I could see in the distance with my ultimate health at the metaphorical peak and I was heading straight for it.

The time went slowly to meet the LLND, but I was happy to finally have some improvements and hope. On the day of my first appointment, my mom drove us down. I needed her to help me with memory, and since the drive was so long, that was a big help too. I wouldn't be able to do that without help or I'd be sleeping in the car on the way back.

Sitting in the quiet waiting room, the phone rang continuously. It was obvious that many people were looking for help to heal their Lyme disease or to find out if that is what they had in the first place. I had to fill out a packet of paperwork, luckily my mom helped with that because it was hard for me to read. Then they called me in and I finally met the LLND. My mom and I sat facing the doctor who sat behind his desk. He looked over the records that had been sent. He asked me a few questions about how I was feeling, what I had been through, and any treatments I had taken. He explained that a doctor is a teacher, and that he was there to help educate me about my body and what was happening. And he asked, "Do you believe you can get better?" I said that I did believe that I could get better. He explained that it would be up to me. He had seen many people in my position, some even worse and they had gotten better. He would not take me on as a patient if I didn't believe I would get better. He made note of how I walked and that my speech was slurred and wondered how I'd been diagnosed and treated right away, but ended up in this position.

During the meantime, I had begun going to my sister's meditation classes to try to ease my mind. It helped me to be around a small group of people who knew me, and who I knew. One day she had a guest come in who mentioned someone that I might be interested in meeting. She said he lived close to the land and had several earth lodges. People would travel from around the world to come see him. She encouraged me to give him a call. His name was Ray Reitze. So I went home and looked up his website. I found him on a website called Heart Teachings with Old Turtle. Once I found the number, I wrote it down on a small piece of paper. Every once in a while, I would pick up the piece of paper and look at it. But I was too afraid to dial the number. Finally something pushed me to dial. The phone rang several times and then an answering machine turned on. Relieved that I didn't have to talk with anyone, I left a message saying that a friend gave me his contact information and had encouraged me to call. I left my name and phone number so he could get back to me. I didn't hear back, as I expected, and somehow felt relief in not having to talk with someone new. It was a struggle to physically talk and to hold my concentration for a conversation. This would leave me exhausted every time.

A few weeks later we had found that Ray would be speaking in Brunswick, Maine. I met my sister Lisa and we went to the event together. It was held in a cozy small yurt. We sat in a circle of comfortable chairs. Ray Reitze came in and they began the circle. Ray wanted to go around and have everyone say why they were there. I was a little uncomfortable with the idea, but the circle went around and when it got to me, I began to speak. As soon as a few words came out of my mouth, Ray lit up and said, "That's you!" He explained that they had received my message, but the phone number I left was the wrong one. They had tried calling me several times. I can't believe I left the wrong number—well with my memory how it was it didn't actually surprise me. After the circle Ray invited me up to the property where him and his wife Nancy lived. He said they had a teaching lodge and he held a philosophy class once a month.

31. Old Turtle and the Earth Lodge

Several weeks went by and still committed to finding out if Ray could help me, I drove an hour north on the highway before turning off onto a road that took me across the country. Driving by the rolling hills, I noticed they were bright green with summer foliage. I watched for the "pick your own blueberries" sign on the side of the road near a barn as explained in the directions I found on the website. Parking my father's truck near the main road I locked it, unsure exactly where I was going. Then I wandered up the long dirt road by foot, over the rocky creek, and alongside the waving grasses that grew tall at the edge of the dirt. The air was warm, a gentle breeze was blowing across the fields, and only the occasional song from the birds to break up the sound from the grasses moving in the wind. A beautiful tree, seemingly perfect, stood in the field to my left, illuminated by the golden sun. I was anxious and feeling nervous not knowing what to expect of this "philosophy class" I was going to.

Someone driving up the road stopped and rolled down their window. "Are you going to Ray's? Would you like a ride?"

"Yeah...yes" I stuttered as I climbed in the passenger seat. The driver offered me fresh berries from an oversized basket. We talked as we made our way up the bumpy road, finally parking the car in the grass where the dirt road ended.

We walked casually around the outside edge of the field, slipping through some trees to another small clearing. The smell of the wood smoke escaping the chimney led us to a mound of earth. This was a structure almost hidden into the land with a living roof. The structure was built of stripped logs piled, laid precisely, and tied sturdy. Dirt harvested from the local area surrounding the mound, covered the roof. Plants were not only growing from the roof, but thriving—further blending the structure with its surroundings. We pushed the small wooden door open and bent down to peek our heads in. Seeing warm smiles, we entered the slightly smokey room. There were several chairs and a few people sitting enjoying the warmth of the wood stove. It was very quiet and peaceful, a soft roar from the stove and random crackling. Sitting in a camp-style chair I settled in, feeling a calm I hadn't felt in a long time.

After a short while a small man named Ray began to speak. "What are you here for?" he asked quietly, yet openly, to the circle. My mind immediately went to, "Don't look at me, I don't want to speak, I don't know. I don't know why I am here." My body tensed.

Around the circle, each person spoke in turn and seemed to know why they were there and spoke beautifully and eloquently. When I realized it was my turn, I immediately felt a knot in my throat. Trying to hold back my body shook slightly until tears streamed down my face. I realized at that moment that I felt so disconnected from myself, from people, and the earth. Sobbing, I tried to hold back the tears that were inevitable.

Ray waited a while and let me be. Everyone sat quietly. I felt their compassion in their silence, something I had never really felt or witnessed before. It was hard to be in that silence, to sit there feeling my own pain. Then Ray asked, "Do you want to do some healing today?" Between sniffles and wiping my nose on the back of my hand, I managed to get a, "Yes….please" out of my mouth. My response came out the opposite of how I felt. I knew at that moment exactly why I was there.

Ray explained that I just needed to mend some broken roots. I slowly sketched on a piece of paper as he spoke, trying to stay present. With the Lyme disease it had affected my thinking and my speech. I was afraid I wouldn't be able to understand, or would look stupid in front of these people whom I just met. I focused by feeling the weight of the pencil on the paper, the comforting drag of running the lead across the page kept my thoughts at bay and my ears open.

"What did you want to be when you grow up?" He asked gently, now standing with his arms up and hands on one of the beams of the lodge. As I spoke, I drew unconsciously, trying so hard to focus. My drawing was more like scribbles, or doodles. When we were speaking he said, "Yes, like that" as he motioned to my drawing. I looked down to see I had a half of a tree drawn. The roots, core, and branches were clearly defined on one side of the tree, yet the other half was absent. He pointed out that this is exactly what would happen if a tree had damaged roots. The branches would be affected. And that day we began to explore my roots.

By the end of the session Ray asked, "Why don't you just go do what you want to do?" When I heard these words, it occured to me that I actually didn't know that I could. And so I left the lodge and Ray that day with a question. "What do I want to do?"

32. Following the Signposts on the Path

R ay Reitze, and as many people know him as "Old Turtle," or simply Grandfather, had helped me to follow my "heart" or what I would call following my spirit. After leaving the earth lodge that day, I began searching for what it was that I really wanted. I had been so focused on becoming a wilderness guide and working toward being a caving instructor and mountaineer that when that was no longer a possibility, I had lost all direction in my life. The illness took over and my focus became survival and seeking desperately for my health.

I received an invitation to go on a women's nature retreat in Western Maine and the opportunity spoke to me. An invitation arrived in my parents mailbox, and as I pulled it out, it sparked an interest. Up until that point all of my wilderness experiences were focused on the outer results: being on the top of high peaks, finishing multi-pitch rock climbs, backpacking long trails, or lengthy visits to the wilderness. A women's nature retreat sounded like a very different approach.

I dialed the phone shaking. Anytime I had to speak I became nervous. I was calling to inquire about the retreat and dialed the phone number of Jen, the guide who was listed on the invitation. What if I forgot who I was talking to? Or what we were talking about? What if I couldn't follow the conversation? I had a jewelry show scheduled for the same weekend as the nature retreat so in order to go on the retreat I would have to make a decision and let some things go. After hearing my rather long story and list of fears and concerns, Jen said, "It sounds like you need to fill up your cup." And I knew that I did. I knew I had to return to the wilderness, to deepen my connection with the earth and to get over my fears of being outdoors and being bitten by an infected tick again.

I had planned on selling my jewelry at a craft fair during that time, but she said if I really wanted it, I would find a way and choose what would fill me up the most. After turning it over in mind, and trying to follow her suggestion, I decided the canoe retreat would fill me more than anything. My older sister Lisa, since she was going to be at the same show, offered to set up a table and to sell my jewelry for me while I was away.

A few days before the retreat was going to begin, my car broke down and had to go into the shop. It was going to cost a few hundred dollars which I didn't have at the time so I parked the car until I could afford to have it fixed. Catching a ride from a friend to the woods in western Maine wasn't difficult, and soon I was dropped off in what seemed like the middle of nowhere.

I had considered the retreat would be relatively easy, because we would be sitting in canoes rather than hiking and focused on meditation and gentle yoga. But sitting gave my back a really hard time. After being in bed for so long, I just didn't have the muscles or strength to sit for very long. I was in terrible pain which accelerated through the day. I had decided ahead of time with the guide that I would be going on this trip not being a "sick" person. The illness or the struggle would not be mentioned. I was attending this retreat as a whole person. So when the pain came I tried so hard not to wince or wrinkle my face. I kept a smile and paddled on down the winding twists and turns of the creek. Ten slow miles we paddled and how beautiful it was in the fall foliage.

How was I going to make it? I carried on conversation as best as I could, but even talking at that point exhausted me. I couldn't wait until we got to camp and settled in. My body was screaming to lay down and rest. My nervous system was over-stimulated and overwhelmed (yes even on a wilderness retreat.) I had been living on meat mostly, and this trip was designed for vegetarians. That was definitely a challenge. I kept sneaking off to my sleeping bag in my tent to shovel spoonfuls of almond butter in my mouth hoping my body could turn that into fuel to keep going. The staff were kind and adjusted by cooking me boiled eggs for breakfast. I hadn't eaten grains for months and had felt much better as grains gave my body an immediate reaction. I tried to not stick out or be different. The food I had depended on wasn't the same, and this became noticeable in the small group.

Luckily I had a massage therapist for a tentmate! At the end of the 10-mile paddle, as I was trying to massage my own head to relieve the massive headache, she came over and worked on my neck, shoulder, and back. That night I went to my tent earlier than the others. I crawled inside my sleeping bag and snuggled in. The sand along the edge of the lake made a comfy spot to lay. And I drifted off to sleep, happy to be snug on the earth again.

I woke before the sun and clicked my headlamp on low so as to not wake my tentmate. I jotted down the thoughts and ideas that had been swirling in my head from such a deep sleep. The light of the morning began to grow outside and I knew sunrise would be soon. Slowly I dressed inside my bag before escaping the cozy warmth. I crawled to the edge of the tent, quietly unzipping the door. I slipped outside into the cool, foggy morning air. A perfect fall day in Maine. I sat with my bare feet on the earth, my toes digging into the sand while watching the swirling fog. I couldn't see very far through the mist.

On my healing journey I had begun to pray in the morning. I didn't want anyone to notice me or see what I was doing, or to hear me. I held this secret to myself and didn't share this with anyone. So I began walking along the edge of the lake, feeling my feet on the sand and then walking further. I could feel smooth rocks on my bare skin and followed them out to a point, where the fog still whirled around me.

My body movements created eddies in the fog and the sun began just barely peeking through the thick fog. I could see the glow through the gray mist, pushing its way toward me, yet the dark swirling world was still around me. I closed my eyes and began talking to the world, saying out loud my prayers–everything I wished and dreamed.

I sent those prayers on my breath in the wind and they mixed with the vapor of the breath off the lake. I spoke truly and freely, feeling my bare feet in touch with the cool rocks, pant legs rolled up, and bundled up in layers. My wool sweater and down vest wrapped me in warmth.

When I felt complete, I felt lighter. I felt a rush to my head as if everything in the universe aligned for me that day. I slowly opened my eyes and witnessed the fog disappear. Facing east toward the sunrise, the warmth finally reached my cheeks.

I took a deep breath in, as if breathing in the moment to fill my body with the life and peace that I felt around me. I sat in that feeling, absorbing all that I could. The smell of the lake, and the cool, damp earth. Feeling the tiny grains of sand just beneath my feet. I then looked down at my feet and saw something strange. Between my big toe and second toe, right between the two, stood a long eagle feather, stuck in the sand and standing straight up. I had stumbled upon this in the fog. It felt as though the earth was welcoming me back. Filled with more life and energy than I had had for the past few years, my body felt the warmth of my return back "home."

During the retreat, we were encouraged to ask questions of the trees, yet what I experienced was that we were really asking questions of our deeper selves. I wanted to know how to fully heal. I knew I had a long way to go. Bringing my question to mind, I looked out at the trees. Seeing which one stood out to me, I approached it until I was so close I could put my forehead on the tree. Breathing with the tree I asked my question and waited patiently for the answer. Once I heard the answer, I would seek out the next tree that stood out. Some of the trees appeared to be glowing, while others looked open or curious. I asked three trees the same question and then returned to the group. With the answers I received from my questions, I realized it was time to fly again. My interpretation was that it was time to move out of my parents' home and go out to Arizona where my body could heal with the warmth and sunshine.

After the retreat I felt refreshed, renewed, and ready for the next step on my journey. I received a ride home with some of the participants (since my car still needed repair.) My new friends drove me right to my parents' home. On the way they learned that I made jewelry and so when we got to my parents' house they asked me to take out all of my jewelry so they could bring some keepsakes home with them. I stacked the trays on the trunk of the car and they looked through everything. They loved their Maine sea glass rings and pendants. By the time they drove off down the road toward the airport, they had purchased enough jewelry for me to get my car back on the road. I felt that I was being rewarded from the universe by following my spirit. My "cup" was not only full, it was overflowing.

I had been seeing my LLND for a while now and my symptoms were improving daily. I finally felt strong enough to make a move, or take the next big step in my life and my healing. The day I returned from the retreat, I began planning a trip to Arizona where I would stay for the winter. That would be the furthest I'd been from home since the onset of the illness. My desires were calling me back to hiking in the mountains.

On January 1st that year, just two-and-a-half months after the retreat, my car was packed and ready for the adventure. With premade turkey burgers, homemade sauerkraut, homemade kombucha, and my medications measured and separated in the weekly dispensers, I was ready. At that time I was on a rotation of three different antibiotics and an antimalarial for babesiosis. I also took some supportive supplements for my digestive system and immune system. I had a specific bag dedicated to medications and supplements. Although my LLND kept everything as simple as possible, only adding something new as needed, I did have to carry a lot with me. The plan was to continue to meet with my doctor every few weeks by phone so he could monitor my progress.

I was prepared for several days of travel by car. I was determined to continue the diet that seemed to be working for me at the time. While on the road, I tried to keep everything consistent with how it was at home. I had my sleeping bag handy for naps as I was still very exhausted and would tire easily. I was with a friend who would do most of the driving.

We encountered a few snow storms in Pennsylvania which forced us to make an early stop at a hotel, but the rest of the drive across the country was clear sailing. We went straight to Colorado to stay with friends where I continued to build my online jewelry business so I could travel easily and work when I had energy. My deepest desire was to get back out into the wilderness and connect with the earth again. I had been dreaming and asking myself ways that I could make that lifestyle possible.

Our car engine was destroyed in Colorado one evening and we sat on the side of the road with no heat for several hours. Good thing we had sleeping bags, we crawled inside and waited for the tow truck. We ended up temporarily stranded in Golden, Colorado, but we were able to do a one-way car rental to Tucson, Arizona. So we rented the car and drove as far as we could and camped outside of the city. Once we made it to Tucson, we were able to borrow a Lincoln Town Car to get around. We stayed at the home of a friend of the family.

While living in Tucson I was able to hike every day, gradually building my strength back. I walked every day and hiked in the nearby mountains. Each weekend I would push myself on a hike that was much harder than I thought I could do. I had to turn around on several, and ended up in bed many days after some hikes, but the general trend was better stamina and so I continued. The mountain air was refreshing, while the different plants and animals were inspiring. The views being so much different than Maine, made me feel alive again. After several months of hiking and strengthening my body, I traveled to Zion National Park in Utah and hiked one of the longest trails in the park. It wasn't easy, but I knew it wasn't going to be. I had looked at the map, at the length of the trail and the elevation gain. I also read trail books that others had written and knew that trying would totally be worth it. Step by step, breath by breath I made my way along the rocky switchbacks that zig zagged their way upward. Resting frequently I repeated in my mind "I can do this." Several times I nearly broke down with exhaustion and disbelief, crying at the edge of the trail. But the beauty around me encouraged me to keep going another step and around the next turn. Wiping tears from my cheeks and smudging red dirt across my brow, I continued forward. When I finally reached the top, my breath was practically taken away by the landscape that was revealed over the horizon. The expansiveness I felt was immeasurable. Sitting on the rim of the canyon, looking at the 2,000-foot red sandstone cliffs another layer of accomplishment filled me with joy and new-found hope. I was looking down on a rock feature called "angel's landing" and became aware in that moment that I was experiencing something the doctors said I'd never be able to do. I had returned to the wilderness! My body was shaking and I wasn't sure how I would make it back down to my car, but I was there. I had done it! I lay down on my back and looked out over the canyon catching my breath. Resting my shaking body and feeling the earth's support beneath me. I felt alive, I really felt alive again. To breathe the fresh air, and to see the massive channels of erosion as water carved the rock over thousands of years, my lifetime felt so small and my daily issues all of a sudden seemed so insignificant. And then I thought, "If I am able to do this and to be here, what else is possible?"

While pondering the next direction in my life I began to wonder what I could do, and what I wanted to do. I wasn't sure and so every morning on my walk I would set my intention and then ask the universe for a sign. Not surprisingly, by being confused myself, I only received confusing answers. "Why won't the universe give me a clear sign?" "Please tell me what to do, what direction to take..."

I wandered the landscapes waiting for spirit to tell me what to do. Looking for an outer calling, yet nothing came clearly. I looked at the trees and their expressions, and how each of the cactus stood, each so different in their stature. I was in awe at the expressions of the earth in this new place. Yet nothing guided me toward anything, my curiosity kept me in the joy of the moment.

Then one day as I was resting between jewelry making sessions, my phone rang. I was nervous to answer because I didn't know who it was. "Hello?' I said after picking up my smartphone and sliding the green button. A gentle voice responded back, "Hello" and explained who she was. To me it felt like spirit was calling, a magical moment when the sign finally came and I received the "call." In this case it was a literal call inviting me to participate in an energy medicine training. It would provide healing for me, a way to work through the underlying causes of the illness I was still suffering with. When she shared the price of the course, it nearly knocked me off my bed. But there were ways this could be done and I could try one course and see how it went before committing to the rest.

It was expensive training, and after losing my job and spending all of my savings on my health and medical bills, this posed a huge challenge. I was convinced this training would help me heal and to finally reclaim my life—so I pursued it. Not sure how I would pay, I made the promise that I would figure out the way. I applied for a scholarship, which was awarded to me after writing an essay on what I planned to do with this training. At that time I was focused on me, on my health. This opportunity led me to feel like I could peer into my destiny, grasp a new direction in life, and begin new.

Within a few months, we were leaving warm, sunny Arizona driving toward western Massachusetts. I was dropped off at my very first class to learn about energy medicine practices that were said to be hundreds to thousands of years old. I was nervous and didn't know anyone when I first arrived. I also didn't know what to expect, or even if I'd be able to make it through the days or the first week. I still had considerable pain, fatigue, and attention issues. But there I was, dipping my toes in the waters of a new destiny.

The teachers suggested that I set up a table and display my jewelry for sale during the class. To my surprise, everyone loved my jewelry so much that I made enough money to help me pay for the training and travel required for the next class just one month later in New York. I continued this for two years, building my jewelry business to pay for all seven of the intensive trainings.

33. Energy Medicine & The Wilderness

My energy medicine training brought me to New York and Massachusetts, even out to Utah and California. Q'ero paqos, or Andean priests, came from the mountains of Peru to help us learn spiritual teachings and energy medicine practices over the week-long intensive retreats. Then we would practice these skills working closely with mentors. I committed to the training on the "fast track" which meant I would do all of my training within two years as opposed to the four years that was the typical length at the time. Of course we could go at our own pace and it was largely dependent on my ability to pay for the classes, travel and accommodations.

My experience during my first class was amazing. I'm not sure I can even put it into words but after a week of exploring the stories that kept me from creating a reality that I dreamed of, I felt lighter and freer than I have ever before. During one practice session I breathed and released, oxygenating my body while the practitioner guided me to look at my thoughts and ultimately imagine myself completely healed. This took about a half hour I would guess, although time completely slipped away. I began to feel my body buzzing, and slowly opened my eyes. Then I walked outdoors barefoot. As I walked along the grass I could hear each blade of grass as though it were singing and I could physically see it's vibration. And each blade was slightly different than the next in sound and how it looked, and somehow I could feel all of it! The rocks were the same as if they were singing with the other rocks both as individuals and as all the rocks together and they sang along with the plants. It sounded so good, and my body buzzed with it. As I walked the path, I crossed over a small stream. The water was also vibrating, sounding its own song that I could see, hear, and feel and the whole earth was singing to me. My body felt so amazing, something I had never felt before. It must have been what some call bliss. I had no pain and no worries. Laying on my back I felt supported by the earth and looked up at the blue sky and the sun. This stayed with me for more than three days.

Returning to Maine after my first class in energy medicine, I began studying with several Master Maine Guides in the northern Maine woods. I was ready to return to guiding in the wilderness, although it couldn't be the same as I had done before. The pain and weakness returned. The fatigue returned and yet I had "tasted infinity" as my teachers described from similar situations.

I learned about guiding canoe expeditions the way the Maine Guides did it and helped on several canoe trips—eventually building up the courage to take the test and become licensed to guide wilderness trips in Maine. Maine is one of the few states that requires a license to guide in the wilderness and I was ecstatic when I finally had the license to guide in the wilderness again...but the question was, "How will I do this?"

I began with small trips, just one on one. A woman traveled from New York to Maine to learn about the energy medicine I had studied and to play outdoors in the lakes and forests in Maine. We both enjoyed the weekend so much! I then led several small weekend adventures in energy medicine and wilderness and offered weekly classes at the local parks and natural areas. My energy was returning as my passions merged and I found a new purpose.

And then finally I was ready to go bigger. It was November 11, 2012, just over 6 years after the initial onset of my illness. I had been planning for quite some time: researching, imagining, and doing what it would take for me to be in full alignment with my bigger dream. The day came when it was time to launch my project out into the world. I had fewer than 100 followers on my Facebook page, and a pretty small but very interactive newsletter list. With the touch of a button, my invitation went out to the "world." I had officially planned and launched my first spiritual wilderness retreat. I was ecstatic!

It felt like it was bringing all of what I loved together in one place, and it felt more "me" than I had ever felt before. The wilderness, the outdoors, hiking, camping, and cabins all in one. I had led many wilderness trips and worked with many groups and weekend workshops, but this would be my first ever to lead a full-on retreat and it would take place in one of my favorite places in the world, Sedona, Arizona!

As much as I had prepared, I wasn't ready for what was to come. The participants began arriving at our small group camping area wearing big smiles. They were dropped off with me for an unknown adventure and they were all very excited. We ate lunch together outdoors at the picnic tables and took the time to get to know each other. Many were coming from Maine and many I already knew in some capacity yet they had not met each other, and a few came from other areas.

I quickly noticed that my introduction and welcome to the group was taken over by the volunteer who had offered to help me with cooking. I started to feel a little uneasy, but I let it go. I thought, "She is probably just excited." But then with each thing I shared and each teaching I brought, she added to it, or tried to change what I said, or clarify what she thought I had meant. I realized we were not on the same page at all. I had asked her for help with cooking and she had agreed to do that, but now it felt like she was trying to run my retreat. So I mentioned to her that I just needed assistance with cooking.

The next morning we got up and spent some time in the morning exploring the area and getting to know the giant trees and the nearby creek. Only then did I bring the group to my favorite place. Everyone wanted to ride in my car, but we had to take two cars because we wouldn't all be able to fit into one.

After sight-seeing we went to a beautiful picnic area for a quiet crystal bowl meditation and casual lunch. My volunteer asked to talk with me and walked me aside saying that I looked tired, and that I should sit and rest. She would take care of lunch and everything. I did sit aside, but only for a short time, it just seemed so weird. I actually was more excited than tired and wanted to spend time with my group, note away from them.

That night after dinner and the group fire, she approached and said she wanted to talk with me. We sat in the camp chairs outdoors by the fire. It was a beautiful night. The fire crackled as the dry wood burned and the air was cool on my cheeks. She began by telling me she was going to speak to me like a child, because I was like a child and she felt like a mother figure to me. That was surely a strange way to begin! She told me that I was wasting the participants' money, that I wasn't delivering what I had promised to them, I was teaching all from ego, and I was failing. Hearing those words and accusations tore my heart apart. I felt very connected to this group (besides my volunteer) and we were having fun and laughing, how did she even know?

I lay in my tent that night. It was about 30 degrees and I was a little cold, but I was comfortably tucked in my sleeping bag. I loved breathing the cool air, it was so refreshing. I barely slept, though, as I was tossing and turning, rolling over with her words going over in my mind. "Where had I gone wrong?" I searched my thoughts and combed my memories for places where I was teaching from ego or not delivering what I had promised.

My workshops and classes always went by how I felt and what I perceived, and they always went so wonderful in the past. I felt like we were right on track. I had a tentative schedule in my pocket and a list of everything I wanted to cover.

All night I searched through every instance, and every interaction. I searched my soul over, the reasons why I was doing this, what my intentions were, and what I hoped to offer my participants.

I felt kind and compassionate and was sharing what I knew. As the sun rose, and the light began to warm the campground, it became clear to me that she had in fact been projecting herself onto me. She was in ego, she was worried because she didn't trust my guidance or flow. But I was in my element and I knew that.

I think I needed that experience to really make me dig deep and understand the "why" behind what I was offering. Being outdoors and cooking on the campstove was my thing, I felt so at home. So in the morning I asked her if she would leave the retreat. She said she would wait and listen to what spirit was telling her, and I thought, "Huh? I've asked you to go, it's my retreat."

She stayed back at the camp that day while the rest of us piled into the Kia Sportage. We fit exactly, all seven of us, and we went off on a joyous ride and adventure around the Red Rocks of Sedona where we could have fun, learn, and explore. We returned later in the day ready to prepare dinner. The volunteer and her friend had already packed and were gone and the incredible relief I felt left me feeling wide open and also vulnerable.

We gathered in a circle and all talked about the experience from our perspectives. I shared my thoughts and feelings, and what I had been going through and how I had been second-guessing myself. Everyone was happy to share their experiences and we all learned from each other. Then I promised to make dinner on the fire and campstove and I told them to take some time to journal and relax.

They all went in different directions and returned as they were ready for dinner. I had been paying attention to the veggies cooking and when I looked back, the rice noodles had turned to mush! The chef in the group got up and offered a hand. Just a quick rinse with cool water and the integrity of the noodles returned. And from there on, we all pitched in to help with meals and cleaning and that made it really fun. We had a great retreat!

All of my clients left the camping area and I began to pack the car. Although it was always hard when everyone was gone, I loved the time after classes when I could really reflect. What an amazing retreat, with amazing people. They left inspired and motivated to make changes in their lives, we made great memories and I brought them into how I experience life--through adventure and exploring earth's natural expressions in different locations. Knowing we will never have this same experience again, I had encouraged everyone to live every moment to the fullest. This experience lit me up so bright! I also learned so much about what I needed for help to do something like this again. I would guide another retreat again for sure!

After my car was packed, I began to drive the curvy roads back toward my home. It was a stunning drive, winding up and out of the desert. After years of absence, my dream of returning to guiding in the wilderness was becoming a reality once again.

34. The Miracles on the Path to Peru

The dream of exploring Peru saturated my mind for many years. Visiting the Andes Mountains was a place I had on my list since first learning about South America in grade school. I knew of a group planning a trip to the Mountains in Peru, feeling pulled to join, I set my intention by placing a $500 non-refundable deposit and officially registering. I knew that I didn't have enough money at the time to pay for the entire trip, but I thought if I really desired it, the ways would simply appear.

But as the time drew near, I realized I didn't have enough to pay for the course, let alone the plane ticket to get there. In my mind, I thought if I desired something, the money would just "show up" especially if the desired action was "right" or "spirit guided." So when this realization came of not having those ways show up, I was disappointed to say the least. Dialing the phone, I contacted the organization to inform them of my situation and my inability to make it this time—that I wouldn't be able to go. The friendly woman on the other end of the phone asked me if I really wanted to go. Excitedly I said, "Yes! Of course I do."

She told me to use the skills I had been learning and anything would be possible.

I had been studying energy medicine through this organization's programs for almost two years and this trip to Peru would be my final course to complete all the requirements for the Certification Program. My learning and experience were about practicing and making decisions based on where I wanted to go in my life, rather than deciding based on the lack or fears I experienced in my past. This could be such an opportunity! So instead of giving up, I made a clear decision and stated it out loud. "I want to be in Peru standing with my bare feet directly on Mt. Pachatusan."

I began to imagine myself there every day. I imagined being on the airplane, flying over the ocean and seeing the expansive land and mountains below. I welled up the feeling of walking off that airplane into a new magical land. I imagined how happy and expansive it felt to be there. I cut out a picture of Machu Picchu and put it in my Mesa, my medicine bundle, and carried that closely to me every day. I would unfold my bundle and take out the small worn piece of paper and look at the image throughout the day. I breathed as if I were there on those mountains everyday. Breathing the imaginary mountain air multiple times throughout the day filled me with hope and possibility. Each morning I dedicated my meditative breathing practice to placing myself in the experience of Peru.

In the meantime, I traveled from Maine to attend an event in Richmond, Virginia that would help me leave the old ways of thinking behind. I knew I had to keep changing the way I thought, to create a healthier lifestyle based on who I wanted to be. I didn't want to be sick, tired or financially struggling any-more, and my desires guided the way.

My Lyme journey was long, and I spent every penny I had trying desperately to gain my health back. Now I was digging deep into my spirit and had the desire to live in a completely new way, from my greatest joy. I just didn't know exactly how to take what was on the inside, what I could see, feel, and imag-ine, and bring that out to become my reality on the outside—to literally step into my dreams.

To get to Peru I would need a lot of help. I had less than 2 months to do this. I hired two coaches and committed to pay-ing them about $16,000 to help me grow a successful business. I was looking at growing a business combining my new energy medicine skills and wilderness guiding in a new way. That way I could experience Peru, and then go even further to other places I dreamed of and imagined. It might not make sense now reading this, but that is what I did because that is what I felt was right at the time.

Every day as I dreamed about the mountains in Peru, I asked out loud, "How can I get myself to Peru? What can I do in this moment to help me take a step closer?" As soon as an idea came, I acted on it. I sold all of my jewelry supplies, tools, back stock, storage, and displays. I sold everything that I could from my simple jewelry business to friends, on eBay, Craigslist, and Etsy. I sold running sneakers I didn't wear any more. I offered energy medicine sessions and my clients happily paid $200 for each session or $500 for a series of sessions. With daily dedication, and imagination, things started to come together.

One day, a woman I had worked with in the past called and asked if I had any classes she could take. I said no during that phone call because I wasn't teaching any classes at the time. After hanging up, I thought about it. "What did she want help with, and why had she chosen to call me?" I called her back and asked her those questions. She wanted help and support to make big shifts in her life and she thought I could help her with that because she had seen what I had done through my Lyme journey. She had followed me through my shift into leading women's retreats. I agreed to help her over a period of a few months. We mapped out the journey and set up a schedule to meet weekly. She was so ready and excited to make these changes, and grateful to have support and help along the way. She asked if she could pay me in cash, and I said, "Of course."

Just a few days later, I sat upstairs in the large sunny office that I had been renting for my classes and sessions. Our plan was to meet here for two full days to get to the root of what she felt was stopping her from "living her dreams." The sun made a square of light on the cream colored carpet. I sat on the floor waiting for her arrival while watching the square move across the room and expand in length.

I heard the door downstairs open and she was giggling as she made her way up the stairs. She turned the corner and sat down with me on the floor. She said, "I brought you all cash and I blessed each bill." Then she spread the bills out in a fan shape around me. She looked up and said with a smile, "There, I have blessed it all so you will continue to receive abundance in your life." It was a surreal moment for me, but it was real. I had been imagining $6,000 in cash in my hands as that would allow me to travel to Peru, and here it was literally spread out around me. And she was giving this to me with a huge smile on her face.

From this commitment, I was able to purchase my plane tickets and secured my trip with the group. I continued my focus with imagining what I would feel like being in Peru. What came up was freedom and expansion so I imagined that everyday. Each day I moved closer to that dream until I was actually experiencing it. I walked onto the plane, sat in my seat and buckled the seat belt. That was when it really hit me, I had done it! I was literally experiencing what I had been imagining! Looking down from the window I could see the ocean and then the mountains. I could see the Andes Mountains from the air just as I had in my mind.

Landing in Cusco, Peru, I was nervous and excited. The elevation was high and immediately made me feel drowsy which lasted for two days. From my bed in the hotel I could hear the people outside, it sounded like a parade, but I was too light-headed to sit up and go to the window to see. The hotel staff brought coca tea which they said would help me to acclimate to the high altitude. It tasted bitter and earthy on my tongue. I couldn't sleep so I lay in my bed half dreaming and half awake. It was a surreal feeling. I couldn't sit up for long, and couldn't sleep well either.

On the second day I made my way to the little restaurant in the hotel. I was not hungry but our guides for the trip had suggested eating something light. Ordering a vegetable soup, I was unsure if I'd be able to eat it, but it was the lightest thing on the menu and seemed the easiest to digest. The warmth of cooked food soothed me and the warm tea settled nicely.

On the third morning I awoke feeling much better. I felt so good I headed down the stairs and out the door for my first real experience in Peru. The people were buzzing. Many approached with kind smiles to offer their weavings and jewelry. I didn't speak or understand Spanish very well, but was able to interact. Many had a great personality and we joked back and forth.

I walked down the street, past the Sun Temple, shimmering gold in the strong rays of sunlight that day. Others who were traveling with me from our group shared some of the history that they knew. There were stories about the Golden Disc that was held in the temple but has since become a legend. We listened and watched the street performers. The bright colors and smiles were very welcoming. I felt great until I had to turn around and walk back to the hotel. That is when I realized that we had been going downhill. Going back uphill proved to be a challenge. It was hard to fill my lungs and feel like I had enough oxygen. But I managed to make it back to the hotel and rest. The following day we would head out to the Sacred Valley.

We visited many of the old temples in Peru. Our guides consisted of local guides, Paqos, and our teachers from the energy medicine school I was attending. The Paqos were simple people, they were considered priests, or spiritual people. They shared their spiritual teachings with us and offered ceremonies at the temples and sacred mountains that we visited. They gifted us with "initiation rites" that were to help awaken our spirit and spiritual abilities that were still sleeping inside of us. We walked to each location with purpose, and with prayer. They taught me how to travel differently up the mountains. Instead of hurrying to the top, we walked slowly, breathing with the mountain. Each step was a prayer. Whenever I was tired or didn't think I would make it, they stopped and in their native language they would thank the earth and the spirits for us getting that far. Then we would continue on. They taught me to ask the mountains for strength.

We were guided up Mt. Pachatusan, one of the sacred mountains, by the keeper of the mountain who explained that the Incas considered this mountain the axis of the world. The mountain stood 15,866 feet in elevation. We took our time climbing and set our base camp part way up the mountain. We slept and ate at the base camp for several days. One morning a small portion of our group got up before sunrise and began to climb the mountain towards its highest peak. While I walked, I prayed. I prayed that I would have the strength to continue and to enjoy the journey. It had been an incredible task just to get me here and I wanted to experience all that I could. We took several quiet breaks. At one point I stopped and took my shoes off.

Then I stood barefoot looking out at the world around me. The tall rocky mountain peaks were dusted with white patches of snow that extended to the horizon in all directions. A few scattered purple bursts of wild lupines caught my eye as they danced gently in the wind. The soft breeze blew wisps of my hair that bounced and tickled the edges of my cool, smiling face. I felt so open and free.

I realized that I had physically stepped into my dream. I could feel a buzzing vibration and the sweetness of this memory I was creating. This is exactly what I had been imagining.

I noticed that the earth wasn't cushy like it was back at home in the Maine forest, or soft like the sand at the ocean's edge. This land was very dry, thirsty, and hard. The rocks were sharp and jagged beneath my feet. The plants were small, crisp tufts. The connection between my bare skin and the earth comforted my entire body, relaxed my nervous system, calmed and opened all of my senses, and held me in complete bliss.

My vision became blurry with the tears that welled up, and my throat clenched. This felt like a dream, and this exact moment was to me, a miracle.

35. The Hope of Destiny

Returning to Maine from Peru was a challenge. In Peru the people were friendly and open. It was a different way of life and I really enjoyed it. I enjoyed Cuzco and also traveling and camping in the mountains. When I came back to Maine it felt like coming home, but that I wasn't really fully connected to this area. I signed up to go out to Utah to take two more classes in energy medicine, to deepen my skills with master classes.

I flew out of Portland, Maine, not sure what I was getting myself into. I had been focused on trying to eat "clean." With the six or so years with active Lyme disease (I was also diagnosed and treated for Babesia, a blood parasite) and the years of antibiotics, I had become very aware of what I put in my body and how my body reacted. This always seemed to change a little bit. At this point in my life I was juicing veggies and eating a lot of fresh and raw foods. My digestive system was beginning to work again. However I wasn't sure what I would find in Park City, Utah.

I was going through security at the small airport in Portland, Maine. They pulled me aside to have a look at the contents of my bag. The security had me stand off to the side. People were still checking their items through. Carefully they unzipped the small carry-on suitcase. "What is this?" "Oh that is my juicer." "This is the first time we have ever seen this go through the line!" They put everything carefully back as they found it and zipped up my suitcase. "You are all set to go." Okay phew, I had tried to look up the regulations for carrying kitchen appliances on the plane, and I was pretty confident it would be alright.

The truth is, I was afraid to go anywhere and not be able to eat what my body was used to. If I didn't have the nourishment I might need, then how would my body respond? Would I be able to think? Would I be exhausted? I had also carried most of my food with me to snack on which included raw food bars, powdered green drinks, and dried meats.

Arriving at the hotel, I unpacked my juicer and met my roommate. We were under the impression the rooms had kitchen stuff, but we couldn't find it anywhere. So on the next trip to the natural food market, we purchased a few knives, cutting boards, and utensils. Just enough to get by. I was on a definite budget, and Park City was a little pricier than Maine. I actually wasn't sure I'd have enough money to buy meals all week! So half way through the first week's class, I suddenly felt called to stay another week for the second class.

I immediately changed my flights with an added fee and made the commitment to stay. I would need to figure out how to make this all work. It had been working up to this point, so I knew I was capable of it. Then I was on the public transit and a few friends from another class I had been in jumped on. They had an Airbnb and invited me to sleep on the couch. Splitting the rent was so reasonable, I checked out of my other hotel immediately. I had begun to believe that whatever I wanted to do,

I would be able to. I would need to desire it, then imagine it, and ask for the next steps to unfold. And step by step I made my way.

In one of the classes we were asked to go outside and choose a place on the earth to work with. I walked down the sidewalk in Park City. I had wanted a nature place, but not too far from the retreat center. I saw a tree planted between the sidewalk and the road and walked over to it. This feels like a good place.

A dusting of snow covered the earth. With my feet I stomped out a circle in the snow. We were asked to put things that came up, or things we were working on inside that circle. So I looked around and picked up a piece of bark. I filled myself with my intention and with my breath, I blew that intention into the bark and then set it down inside the boundaries of my circle. I repeated this until I felt that all of the things that were popping up into my conscious mind from my subconscious were held by the earth and seen by my own eyes. Relief washed over me seeing that the earth was helping me to hold all of this. It wasn't just me anymore.

I took a couple of steps back toward the retreat center when something caught my eye. It was a piece of paper that clearly said, "Wake Up!" I bent over to get a closer look and picked it up—how perfect it was! I set that in my circle on the earth with the attention to become more fully awake to my inner thoughts and to the world around me.

Feeling complete, I walked back into the retreat center. We had a lunch break, so everyone was milling about and enjoying their meals and snacks. They allowed me to set up my jewelry (I still had leftover jewelry from before I went to Peru) and crystals on one of the tables, so I went to check to see how my sales were doing. The sales were sure helping me to buy lunch and cover expenses!

I sat in the back of the room and our class was well over ninety people. We began the next session. The teachers asked us to share our experiences. So as those who felt called to share, stood up and were handed the mic, each shared what they had learned during the last exercise.

One older gentleman stood up and began speaking. He said, amazed, "I found this piece of paper on the ground with a message. It said 'Wake Up!' I thought that was perfect." When those words hit my ear, I giggled inside, having an idea of the paper coffee cup sleeves, as I had seen one also. How curious! And then he continued to share how amazing that experience and the message was. I thought it was neat that we both had found the same message.

After the session we were asked again to visit our spaces outdoors and when I got to that tree that was holding my space, I looked around and my circle was nowhere to be found! The warmth from the sun radiated from the earth and melted the snow. My circle was gone, the boundary I had stomped out was gone. The paper that said "Wake Up!" was gone, and all my problems were gone too!

From that experience I thought about creating strong boundaries in my life. I also felt like, well if someone else wants to take my problems then go for it, ha! I don't need them.

36. The Invitation to TEA'S

While I was at the retreat in Utah, I felt a strong need to turn on my phone. It was an unusual feeling for me at an event like that, however, as we were working with "retrieving our destinies," I thought it would be in my best interest to follow my feelings.

I opened my email to find an invitation to "tea time" and storytelling in Falmouth, Maine. There was a man speaking, a storyteller from the Mi'kmaq Nation who had been traveling across Canada and the US speaking, and he was going to be sharing spiritual teachings in the town next to where I grew up. This was unheard of!

The invitation encouraged everyone to reserve a space. This opportunity was only open to eight people and I knew I had to be one of those eight! Immediately I hit "reply" and typed a message on my tiny phone screen saying that I would like to come. I tapped the "send" button, hoping that I would be one of the first eight people to reserve my seat for this amazing and once-in-a-lifetime opportunity. I then shut off my phone, tucked it away and continued my retreat.

I was immersed in a two-week training on what they called "destiny retrieval" and we were learning ways to track energy out into the future to change our momentum in life. This, the instructors explained, would help us to consciously create the life that we really wanted. How would we know this worked? But we practiced imagining the best life possible. Then we practiced seeing and letting go of the patterns that held and bound us to what we didn't really want. All of the ceremonies that were taught to us and that we practiced were ancient teachings that originated in Peru. These were taught and shared by Q'ero Elders as part of the prophecies they spoke of and the changing of the world during our current time period. After this very intensive class, I returned back home to Maine.

I remember walking with a client through the forest soon after my return. We meandered our way over a mountain as we headed toward the beach. The path brought us through the trees up over a hill to an amazing lookout spot at the top of a rock cliff. We could see the beach and some rolling waves far below, and the shape of a snake where the tidal river flows back and forth. I could see Mount Washington clearly in the distance, even though it was just a speck of white on the horizon.

As we sat there a shadow from above graced us, a turkey vulture circled. It flew so close I could have reached out and grabbed it with my hand. It was suspended there just above us, in the wind. We enjoyed our snacks and then headed down to the beach. Playing on the rocks in the sand, moving and stretching and splashing in the waves, we laughed. She was there to make some major life changes and had asked for my support. We lay on the rocks in the sun and began to imagine.

When we were complete we began the walk back, barefoot on the path. This was to create a stronger connection with the earth, literally. We laughed, skipped and explored each plant on the two-mile hike back to the parking lot. The day was perfect and the experience left me feeling light and happy. I dropped her off at her car where we had met early that morning, and headed back to my parent's home. I quickly showered, grabbed a quick bite to eat, made up a yerba mate tea, and headed out the door to my black 1993 Volvo 240, also known as "The Tank."

I drove up the winding road on Route 88 toward Falmouth with the sparkling ocean to my left. I barreled along in my "tank" toward the home of someone whom I didn't yet know. In fact, I was more than a little anxious. The GPS on my phone alerted me that I had arrived. I pulled off to the right of the road in a small sandy pullout just before the road took a bend. I took out my phone, confirmed the address with the email. There were second thoughts running through my mind, "Maybe I shouldn't go, maybe this was a bit crazy since I didn't know who lived in this house, and maybe I should just go home and enjoy the sunny summer afternoon. After all, I don't even know anyone who will be here."

I scrolled a bit on my phone until I built up enough courage to go inside. I entered through the front door, which was a bit of a challenge. There were stools and chairs set neatly in a circle around the small room. There were people milling about, introducing themselves and talking with one another. They quickly greeted me and, because I'm not a social person, this was a little challenging but very interesting. I had never been to such a kind and welcoming gathering. We had tea and cookies and then David Lonebear Sanipass arrived. Dressed in work clothes, a little dusty and covered in paint and dried plaster. He plopped down in the chair saved just for him, while dust escaped his denim pants in a small cloud. Someone brought a warm cup of Red Rose tea out from the kitchen and handed it to him. He looked a little awkward and uncomfortable, but soon he began to speak. Everyone leaned in, wide-eyed to listen except for the one woman who slept while sitting on the floor.

The flicker from the white candle made subtle changes of light and shadow in the room. Each word he shared resonated with me and made connections in my mind that I never thought of or made before. The words were familiar. He shared his life experiences of growing up in Northern Maine, and what it took for him to get there. I sat and listened for three hours. The suggestion I heard was to go out and shake someone's hand next to you and to find out their name. There were many more, but this one stood out because he used me as an example during the talk since I happened to be sitting right next to him. As the "tea time" closed, the announcement came that there would be another "tea time" with David at the same place in one week.

I cleared my schedule and made sure I would be able to attend as many of these "teas" as possible. At first there were only a few scheduled, but since people were listening, David was allowed to share more and more, and soon we had two "teas" every week.

The community quickly outgrew the eight-person minimum, and we expanded to upwards of 60 people crammed in the small house trying to peer through the walls to hear these ancient teachings. I attended every "tea time" I could. After each gathering a wave of excitement would hit the community. As we gathered, met each other, and listened, we carried this excitement out into our worlds and everyday lives and back into the "tea time" again. The energy that I felt from these gatherings was amazing. It was palpable, I actually left there with my body buzzing. I couldn't wait to go out, to find new ways of connecting with people, experience the earth in new ways, and share this new and rediscovered way of living. Later we would find out that these ways of holding circles were actually called TEA'S. This was an acronym for Time, Earth, Air, Space.

37. Three Days Out

After about 4 or 5 months of attending the TEA'S, I felt like I was hitting a wall in some sense. My excitement had jump-started my passion to live and explore, and to push my boundaries on all levels, but there was something more. I walked through the woods every morning inspired now to get up early to watch the sunrise and to walk beside the river while observing the sunset. It was said that our prayers could be heard more during those times. That the magnetic field of the earth changed during those moments. So I wanted to find out.

It was during these walks that I realized that connection with the earth that I had before was there, but only limited to the paved or well-traveled paths. I didn't venture far, and yet I felt that feeling well up inside of me. Feeling so deeply inside me, I knew I really needed to return to the wilderness. I needed to go back by myself. Up until that point I had gone on small hikes, but I had someone with me. Could I still trust myself in the wilderness? Could I still make a fire? The desire to unplug from social media and the internet and to go back into the wilderness grew stronger and stronger inside me.

David had asked after one of the TEA'S, "How can I help you?" I had turned this question over in my mind until I woke up one morning and I knew. I built up the courage to finally ask, "Hey, I think I know how you can help. Can you help me find a place to go out in the wilderness for three days?" He said, "Yes, I can do that," and informed me that he would get back to me. I was anxiously awaiting the next steps. "Maybe I should just go find a place myself," I thought. But a few days later, David sent latitude and longitude coordinates. With these coordinates, I was able to pinpoint the location on a topographic map. It looked like an interesting area and it wasn't too far away. I was excited, and scared at the same time. It had been years since I spent a night alone in the woods, let alone three full days. We agreed on the dates, it would be just about a week and a half away.

I then gathered all the things that I thought I might need. As the day got closer I went through everything and packed my backpack with what I thought would be essential. My desire was to re-enter the wilderness and to feel confident in my abilities. I wanted to know that I could do it again. It was the end of January and just barely above 5 degrees Fahrenheit. I was nervous, but also ready to get out there again. Why did this feeling begin in the dead of winter? In sub freezing temperatures?

In preparation I visited Ray, Old Turtle, before heading out. We talked about where I was in my life and how far I had come. He reminded me to be like a magnifying glass, to be the lens that focuses the light clearly and perfectly on what I wanted going forward. He said my focus had been behind me. I didn't realize it until then, but I had been focusing in the wrong direction by focusing on the past. This was an opportunity to really focus on the future.

In addition to the wilderness trip, we talked about the invitation I received from David to speak at one of the upcoming events. I didn't know if I could get up and speak in front of so many people. David hadn't given any direction on what to talk about, it would be whatever I chose. Things were definitely changing for me, and I could feel it. I felt moved to step more fully into who I had dreamed of becoming. And this was not at all easy!

After talking with Ray, I felt more confident about the reason to head out to the wilderness, and more confident in my ability to be able to give helpful information to others simply by sharing my own journey.

So I said good-bye for the time being, walked down the long driveway and headed out. On my drive back home I was slowed down by a bus ahead of me. And then a car pulled in front of me and drove extra slow, slow enough I had to put on my brakes. "How can I ever get anywhere? This is ridiculous," I thought. Then it occured to me that this car was probably slowing me down for a reason. I looked for bumper sticker messages and my eyes caught sight of the license plate. The license plate read, "3DAYSOUT" and I thought, "Seriously, no way!!" That is exactly where I am going. That is so funny. I was planning on going three days out into the wilderness. Just after this realization, a car passed both of us with a license plate that said "UTEACH." And although they were license plates on cars and probably meant something to their owners, I took them as personal messages from spirit. I had to be in the right place at the right time to receive these in this exact moment. So I decided, "Yes I am going to do this."

I had been staying at my grandmother's house while she was away in Florida. Sitting with my pack packed, I watched out the sliding glass doors for the truck to arrive. I could see water begin to drip from the icicles and some fog begin to lift from the settling snow. The needle on the thermometer was slowly rising. This seemed like a good sign, and eased my mind slightly.

Soon the silver truck rounded the corner, emerging from the cedar trees and pulled into the driveway. David came in and checked the weight of my pack (making a few comments on the heaviness) and asked me a few simple questions. He made sure I "had everything I would need." I threw my pack in the back of the truck, jumped in the front, and we headed toward the woods. I was so nervous as we pulled into a gas station. While David filled up the tank in the truck, I sat inside the cab thinking about this adventure. I hoped I would be ok. I really had no idea what the terrain was like where I was going besides what I had found by looking up the coordinates and looking at a topo map of the area. I could see potential for water and there appeared to be some relatively flat places to camp.

Soon again we were driving up a winding road I didn't recognize. There was a small pullout near a telephone pole and David said, "This is it" as he pulled in. David dropped me off at a trailhead off the main road and told me to stay off the trail and out of sight. Pretty easy to do with a big red heavy back-pack! The snow was deeper than my boots, since I only had regular leather hiking boots at the time. I sank about knee deep into the fluffy, cold, white snow. But I trudged my way through the woods looking for the small creek that ran down from the mountain. I could see it by the contours in the land and headed straight for it.

I definitely wasn't in the kind of shape I used to be. But the quiet woods, the birds, and the fresh air had me feeling alive and free. When I reached the creek I found that it was frozen solid on the top. Following the flow downhill I listened to see if it would be possible to collect water. About a hundred feet down, I began to hear the song of the trickle of moving water so I found a flat somewhat open place where the warm sun shone through the trees. This would be a good place to set up my small camp. My backpack dropped with a thud.

From my new camp, I could hear the trickle of the water as it flowed over and under the ice. I made my way toward it and then, with one step, my foot disappeared up to my thigh in deep thick mud. I tried to pull my foot out. I could hardly move it, and my other foot began to sink. I was being swallowed by the earth in the first few minutes of being back in the wilderness. What ran through my head—well, looking back—was quite hilarious. I was thinking I would have to turn on my emergency phone, call David, and get evacuated from the situation.

However, I was able to remain calm and got my body positioned in such a way that I could slowly pull my legs out. Hopefully no one was around to see this. I had lost one boot deep in the mud, and stuck my hand in to see if I could reach it. A mix of mud, slush, and snow soaked into the sleeve of my shirt underneath my coat. I had to have the side of my face on the ground just to reach down that deep, and I began to pull on that boot. There was a sucking sound and then with a loud popping noise it came free.

Wow, so now I am covered in mud, wet, and it's the middle of winter in Maine. I filled my water bottle in the creek and crawled up to a small sitting place in the sun. I had to roll my wet socks off my feet and peel my pants off my legs. There I stood in my long underwear, wet and muddy. Luckily I knew from experience, they would dry quickly.

I gathered a tinder bundle of natural dry fibers, some very small twigs, and prepared a fire. Then I took out my flint and steel that I brought with me. It had been years, but the flint and steel would likely be much quicker than making a bow drill friction fire. Setting myself comfortably in the sun, striking the flint with the steel, I sent sparks down into the tinder bundle. I was surprised to see the embers glowing orange in just a few tries, it had been so long since I had tried. The glow grew and with a slight breath, soon I had tiny flames. I built the small fire up gently and slowly but quick enough as to not lose that opportunity.

My small stainless steel cup was next to me at the ready. It was completely black on the outside from sitting on many fires. It had warmed many cups of tea and coffee, and even soups for me. After the little fire was burning pretty hot, I moved the sticks around to make a small nook where I placed the cup with water from the creek. I watched the smoke rise and spiral around just above me, just as the sun shone through, spreading rays across the opening where I sat. Soon I could hear the bubbles as the water began to boil. I felt at home. Sitting by the fire waiting for a warm cup of tea, I dried my pants and socks and cozied in for my three days out, solo. It is interesting that it warmed up to above 50 degrees with warm rain, just for the three days I was out. Then the earth froze again once I was back home.

38. Remembering the Earth's Vibration

My involvement with this community grew and I found myself traveling every week to share the Star Teachings in different areas. We went to New York, Boston, North Carolina, and around Maine. The travels were intense, revealing more of the ancient teachings than I ever imagined possible. The teachings were shared in the car, at the restaurants, and out in the streets. We covered everything from physics to language, and math to kindness. Most of the time, the teachings came without warning, sparked by the curiosity of a question. Many of my notes and diagrams are on placemats with remnants of the mornings breakfast or greasy napkins torn and stained.

While we were traveling David was usually sleeping in the back of the car and the rest of us intently discussing the teachings we heard at TEA'S. I realized then, as we were excitedly "awakening" that sometimes it became really hard to remain in kindness to self, others, and community. To become aware of information that had been hidden sometimes made us confused, and sometimes even angry. Especially when the "awakenings" were about ourselves, but especially when we took them personally unnecessarily.

One day during that summer, I was really mad about something. Something someone else had said (it wasn't even to me or about me). I went for a jog over a small mountain to work it out, to ease my mind that was spinning in circles. The mosquitoes were thick through the damp forest during the early morning hours. I knew if I arrived before sunrise, I wouldn't see anyone else. I ran hard, then slowed my pace only to be eaten alive, so I had to keep moving. The blackfly bites were bleeding around my ankles. I kept moving through the thick and humid air towards the ocean. It felt like torture, and there was nothing I could do but to keep moving.

I ran as hard as I could and probably ate a thousand bugs on the way while racing to the sandy beach that I knew was on the other side. The flies didn't follow me out of the forest, and I was so happy to finally be able to breathe freely without pursing my lips to filter out the bugs. As soon as I hit the sand, my shoes came off to dig my bare toes into the soft granules.

The tide had recently changed and was moving back out to sea, but it left the sandy earth damp. And with the heat of the day, the water evaporated into a thick mist and the sun glowed majestically through the low foggy cloud.

I made my way to a circle created by the granite bedrock. I lay down on my back supported by the hard, wet, sand and I began to sing my favorite chant. My song was directed toward the sun, the moon, the earth, and my place in this universe. After a while, my teeth began to vibrate and then it moved to my jaw and my head. Then my back on the sand began to vibrate as well and soon my body began to buzz all over.

I stopped chanting and the vibration continued. Not only could I see it, but I could feel it. The vibration of each tiny grain of sand and each rock sounded so beautiful singing in harmony with those around it. I could see and hear the vibration of the water droplets in the mist and the sun shining through. I could hear the song of the earth and I could feel it.

Soaking in this moment for what seemed like only minutes, I found myself hours later, still in wonder and awe. I held a sense of renewal and a deeper connection to who I really am. I walked back over the mountain and through the woods, ready for the next adventure.

39. A New Way to Experience the Earth

Sometime in the first few months when I was at my sickest I asked out loud to myself, "When will I get better?" Laying in my bed, unable to sit or stand, I lay on my back with weights on my ankles. Telling my legs to lift one at a time, attempting to will my inner strength. My leg would rise a few inches off the floor, my body shaking uncontrollably, it would drop back to the floor. A few lifts and I was exhausted.

When I asked again when I would get better, I saw a flash of an image of myself with long hair pulled back and I was wearing all white. My hair was pretty short at the time so seeing this, I knew it would take a long time for me to actually get there. But I held that image in my mind, returning to it daily and slowly moved toward it, that image was what I imagined to be myself in full health.

When I was five years old, I saw a program on TV and watched martial artists of all ages move in such beauty. How were they able to move their body like that, like a dance? Each year following I would watch the demonstrations at the local festivals. And each year I wanted to try it myself. But what stopped me?

It wasn't until I was very sick and recovering from Lyme disease, that I actually stepped foot inside a dojo. A dojo is a place to practice the way, a place to gather and learn. I was in neurological rehabilitation to manage the brain damage that had occured with the Lyme infection. It had left it difficult for me to walk, to write, to stand, or even communicate. The brain injury support group that I was a part of was invited to practice tai chi at a studio in Portland, Maine.

I remember my first time stepping foot into that dojo, it was like entering a beautiful sun-lit temple. Slipping my shoes off, I walked into the naturally lighted room. Giant green plants adorned the corners and the sun shone warmly through the windows. We were greeted by a soft-spoken man, gentle in his mannerisms, who guided us through the practice while most of us remained seated on chairs.

Bringing the energy in from the earth into my body and moving gently back out while flowing and breathing—after 30 minutes, my body and mind were exhausted and I barely made it home. Recovering from this experience, I slept for several days, but I was happy to return the following week. I continued the practice at the studio, and at home. As I built my strength I was able to practice more and eventually to stand. It took about two years of neurological rehabilitation, tai chi, and adaptive sports before I really felt the difference in my balance, strength, coordination and mind. This was all before I went to TEA'S and met David.

One day I arrived a few minutes early to the house where we were going to have a TEA'S and David Lonebear was going to be speaking again. The woman who was hosting the TEA'S was speaking of a class she went to in southern Maine that incorporated the Star Teachings, the teachings David Lonebear was sharing with us, but in a physical form.

David and a student of his had started the class years ago. The host spoke about learning to build fires with "nothing," of hitting a target with an arrow blindfolded, and working together with others in the practice to overcome challenges. When I heard this I said, "I want to take the class." However, that particular class was by invitation only, and I wasn't even close to being in the shape needed physically, let alone mentally or emotionally. But that desire was sparked and I told myself that I would do what it would take to get me there.

My training with the Master began before I even knew. It started as soon as those words "I want to take that class" came out of my mouth. However, I didn't recognize this subtle training until months later. Often I would be standing and David, a Master in the tradition of Sho-Kai, who was also teaching the Star Teachings at TEA'S, would come and bump up against me, and my arms and legs would go flailing as I stumbled sideways. I was, more often than not, completely off guard and ungrounded. I began to recognize this in all areas of my life. While I was standing, while I was walking, and while I went about my usual business during the day I found myself not paying attention to my surroundings or myself. Master Sanipass would come up to me and shake his hands right in front of my face vigorously. It was so annoying, I'd blink, or turn my face. But he would continue to test my reaction over and over.

I began to travel with David Lonebear in 2013 to share the Star Teachings and TEA'S. TEA'S are gatherings to learn and practice the Star Teachings. They are created in a certain way to build community. While traveling to TEA'S from state to state, my lessons would occur without me being able to prepare ahead of time such as while we were walking to the events, or after meals. The training began that day that I asked, and has never stopped.

One day I walked into a home to hear a familiar voice say, "But I don't know if anyone will show up." I immediately knew who was speaking and what he was talking about. "I would!" I responded excitedly. The voice was of Master Sensei Reese, a voice familiar to the TEA'S and I knew I wanted to study and learn the ancient practices. I made a commitment in that moment to go to his weekly classes to learn as much as I could.

We began the following Sunday morning. The preparations I had been previously involved with definitely helped! I had been working with a body, mind, strength trainer who was involved in the Star Teachings as well. She helped me to build the strength that I had lost while I was in bed for so long with Lyme. She helped me to change the way I talked to and about my body, and most importantly she helped me to let go of what I "used to be able to do." My focus became what I currently was capable of, and where I could go with my body, strength, and skills. We started slow, building my core strength, and opening my chest. My shoulders were consistently rolled forward, my back barely able to hold me upright. We worked on standing so I could feel confident, and also to stand properly. Then we moved on to balance and overall strength.

I remember being inside the small training room, a shed a short distance from her home that she had transformed into a studio. I remember the hard floor, the carpet beneath me. On hands and knees looking forward she would talk about what she called the "saggy horse." And she'd get on her hands and knees with me and show me the "saggy horse" and laugh and then show me what I was supposed to be doing. Pulling the muscles up. "My goodness" I would think, I have become so weak.

She gave me exercise to do at home and I did them religiously. I so desperately wanted to feel better and stronger. Later as my strength and confidence grew, we worked on full body planks. While holding the planks she would often tell me stories that David had told her. I remember her re-telling The Woodpecker Story and we would discuss what it meant to us and what we had heard or we would laugh at the recent telling of The Bear Story. I remember laughing so hard about the "jello bear" in that story and pulling the lessons out.

One night I had a dream that felt significant. When I went to her training studio the next day I shared this with her...while doing a plank and struggling not to be the "saggy horse" I explained the dream. In the dream I was hopping over large boulders with her and David. They had given me a small backpack weighing 35 pounds and they expected me to run and jump on these boulders. Then I was instructed to hold a plank position with the backpack on my back, my hands on one boulder, feet on another, and my body bridging the gap. I shared with her how strong I felt and excited to be able to do that someday.

As soon as I told her, she stopped with a curious look on her face. Then she said, "Of course! We're going outside." "Ok great" I thought, I love being outdoors. We went into her beautiful garden area and she had me do planks out there. While holding myself up off the ground with my hands and feet touching the earth, I could look at all the tiny pants and the small red ants that were crawling about. She noticed my strength had changed drastically. "I thought so," she said. "We should have done this earlier."

After that time, we worked on strength training outside by the ocean, in the water, or in the forest. The earth is a source of energy for me, a source of strength. Lifting rocks, doing planks on logs, and hanging from trees became my training. The work and the support built me up so much in terms of strength, but also my inner light. It was fun, and hard.

I trained with her for about a year before reaching a clear peak in my health. I felt energetic, clear, and better than I had in many years. Between the strength training, running, and community support, I felt healthy and ready to begin a family. I had a healthy pregnancy and gave birth to a baby girl in April of 2014. She was born twelve years after the onset of my Lyme disease. My daughter came to this world with a force. She is a beautiful, energetic girl with eyes that shine with curiosity and she has a heart of kindness. All of that prepared me not only physically, but also emotionally, and mentally to begin classes with Sensei Master Reese.

"What do I wear?" I found myself contemplating the morning of the first class. I knew where we would be meeting and that we would be outdoors but that was it, that is all I knew. I had no idea how long we would be out there. I had no idea what we would actually be doing. It was mid-summer, so I wore a comfortable shirt with cut-off sleeves and my favorite pair of lightweight cargo pants that I used to wear while hiking. Pulling into the dirt parking lot I was a little nervous and also excited. I didn't really know what I was getting into. Walking down the wooden stairs to the beach, I could see some people were stretching on the sand, others were moving around, and several of us stood there awkwardly not knowing where to begin. Sensei Master Reese called us over to gather by the water and the class officially began.

Standing on the beach in a circle we closed our eyes. "Imagine that you are holding the last drop of water in your hands" a soft, timeless voice guided us in this visualization. My hands were stacked right at my belly, at my solar plexus, as instructed. I could feel the wind through my hair and the tiny grains of salt as they took flight from the ocean's breath and stuck to my cheeks.

Sensei Master Reese said, "Follow me," and motioned up the beach. The first question that came out of my mouth was, "Can we go barefoot?" "It's your practice," was the response that I received. Well, nothing like putting the learning responsibility on me! I decided to take my shoes that time just in case. I had no idea what we would be doing and didn't want to challenge myself too much unnecessarily. We walked back and forth on the sand at the water's edge learning about the Tiger's Path.

I had asked for this. The practice of Sho-Kai, the energy of water. The first class brought me lessons far more than strength, balance, and clearing my mind. It brought an awareness of myself in this world, in this environment, and in relation to others. The first lessons reminded me of how conversations were coming at me, how sometimes people attack with their words. In the practice people came at us with a fist out. This was held safely, and slowly so we could learn and respond. How can I let those hurtful words move past me rather than striking me? A good lesson to take with me into my everyday life.

I was surprised at the deep messages and understanding I received in the first class. The first class we learned kicks and punches, but first we learned blocks. At the end we moved into the water, with all of our clothes. Front kick, roll (yes under the water) pop back up and turn around. Front kick, front kick, roll... the water goes in my nose and burns my eyes. Pop back up and Sensei Master Reese gets right in the way. "Get out of my way!" I scream inside as I keep going, sand scraping my skin and my clothes hanging heavy with the ocean's salty water.

Master Sanipass looks at me and says, "How is the water?" Those words echoed through my mind and I knew there would be a lot more of this. We were then told to go home. We were asked to practice what we know. Master Sanipass had told us that he could teach us all the Katas and how to kick above our heads but the most important is to, "Practice what you know, kindness, compassion, and happiness." I went home and practiced while my baby was napping. I'd push her in the swing and practice my kicks. Push the baby, kick, kick, push the baby, punch punch. Every moment I had I practiced everything we were learning in the classes. I attended Master Sensei Reese's classes every week as consistently as I could.

The teachings brought a deep understanding of the energy and the flow of life. They matched perfectly and supported the teachings I was learning in the TEA'S. How to move through life with more contentment. I've learned not only how to protect myself with actual techniques, but also strengthened my spiritual fortitude. To keep myself grounded, really connected to earth, and to stand for my beliefs. I've learned how to be at peace with chaos around me. And most importantly how to move to the edge of my comfort, to the edge of my beliefs, and not only to explore that place, but to move all the way through to the other side.

My life's journey took me from feeling connected to this earth, to feeling poisoned and afraid to touch the earth, to an even deeper connection to my true-er self, to this earth, and to this universe.

When I asked David in 2012 if he could help heal me from the last symptoms of Lyme he said, "I can't heal you, then you wouldn't know how to do it yourself." He told me, "Go to the water, fill your hands, and wash your face." Clarifying what types of bodies of water would be most beneficial he then suggested that I ask out loud, "Please take this pain away from me. And from that day on I did.

Looking back, these suggestions got me outdoors, in direct connection with the earth and the water. It was winter and it was cold, and I had to fight for it. To get up early even though I was tired and to go find the water. Then the sting on my face as that cold ocean water was splashed and the winter gusts cooled my face even further. My hands turned red with the cold. But I did it. I had to do something. This is something that he told me his master always said: to change direction, to change anything, you have to "do something," you have to take a step in a new direction. If I wanted my health and my life back, I had to fight everyday, every moment.

40. To Go Beyond

Several years went by. My daughter grew and her father and I went in different directions. I focused on my spiritual growth, martial arts, and traveling to share the teachings that I was learning. I finally felt healthy, happy, and excited for the future.

I find myself barefoot standing slippery wet bedrock at the ocean's edge. I am looking out at the vastness around me. The water extends to the horizon which glows with the reflection of the early autumn sunlight. My body shivers ever so slightly with the cold shocking spray of the waves as they hit the face of the rock below me sending a cold spray upwards.

The incoming tide approaches and challenges my position. I am in a stance, feet spread apart, one leg bent directly under me and one leg extended out to the side. I raise my bo staff—a heavy, long, straight stick—above my head and breathe consciously. I breathe in the ocean's salty breath. I breathe in the smells of the wild roses on the shore and the warm smell of the rocks in the sun. I breathe in the earthy smell of the dirt deposited by wind and water. This fills me with life. The sharpness of the rocks dig into my feet, my legs begin to shake under stress, my arms ache, and David says, "Stay right there, breathe. Keep holding it, breathe." My body and mind sink into the moment. The sun shining a bright white light, the rumble of the ocean waves on the rocks, soothe my thoughts. I see the bright green plants on the edge, moving tenderly in the wind.

We are alone, just the two of us out here on the coast of Maine. Just as I slip into the comfort of the stance and being held by the earth, I hear the roar of a wave approaching...in anticipation, I dig my feet in deeper to strengthen my stance. I take a deep breath. The wave slams the rock and hits me from the back with a force I've never felt before. "Just breathe, keep your eyes open, stay focused." These thoughts stay steady in my mind as the water slams my body and rushes backward, snaking around my legs and feet as it is sucked back into the ocean between swells. The foamy cold water tests my ability. To be grounded in both physical body and mind. I feel a rush of energy inside me like I've never felt before, maybe that is what it feels like to be alive. The edge of fear, in the beauty of the place where the earth meets the sea. I have finally arrived.

Little did I know that this man who had become my best friend in the world, would become my partner and we would marry within a few years.

41. Thoughts on Healing

Healing begins with you. It is more than a desire to do so, it has to be so deep and so true that it drives your physical and mental self to do anything to achieve it. You have to want that transformation so bad you would do almost anything for it. Your drive has to be there in the front and center, day in and day out. It is a fight that you just can't lose. You have to refuse to lose.

You need to be able to continue on when it feels like everything is shattering around you and at the same time be kind and compassionate to your own mind and body. The ability to change your thoughts and actions to align with what you really want is imperative. This takes clarity in knowing yourself and writing down what you want. It takes commitment and practice and to believe it is possible.

The first thing that my doctor asked me was, "Do you believe you can get better?" My doctor said he couldn't help me if I didn't believe it myself. How powerful is that? You have to believe that you will actually do the things that it takes to get better. Those things aren't always easy!

You have to make the commitment, over and over again, every day, every moment through the ups and downs. You cannot stop when you feel more downs than ups.

Make the changes, those small subtle changes and stick with them while always listening to your body, listening to your inner dreams and desires. What are those thoughts that are swirling around in your head? What do you daydream about and don't tell anyone else about? What are those subtle thoughts that you hold so sacred to yourself that you don't dare to share them with anyone else? Those are the dreams you need to listen to if you are going to get anywhere in this precious life. I dare you to listen.

There are changes on all levels. Changes in nourishment and how you fuel your body and mind, mental thoughts, changing perspective, changing your stories, changing your everyday habits. You need to move your body and listen to your spirit. Always go back to listening to the whole being you are. To navigate your life by your inner light and be ok with not knowing everything. And all of this...THIS is just the beginning.

There are many peaks to living your dreams, and also many valleys and paths to travel. That is life, a wave. The greatest gift is to enjoy the journey you are on, because it can change in a matter of moments without warning.

So go find it, go find what you want. Go find what you are seeking. It's right there for you, it's so close you can touch it. Look around and pay attention because it's in your dreams. And all you have to do is recognize it, and ACT in a way that it already exists.

If you can dream it, it is possible!

Acknowledgments

'd like to start by thanking my incredibly supportive husband, David L. Sanipass for encouraging me to share this story and for taking me out on more adventures for photo shoots while dreaming about the book cover. Thank you for your overall support in guidance in this whole process.

A deep thank you to Chantel Purcell for countless hours of editing and proofreading, your encouragement helped me to get over the hump of what seemed impossible.

A big thank you to Larissa Davis for inspiring me to keep going and for all your help with formatting, the technical and beautiful aspects of making this book readable.

I'd like to thank my mom, Linda Ouillette; my dad, John Ouillette; my sister, Leah Webber for the support you gave to get me through; my sister Lisa Jansky; and brother-in-law Paul Jansky for supporting, reading, giving feedback, and the excitement and enthusiasm that kept me going. Thank you to my "Aunnie" Ann Stowell, and my Grammie, Theresa Charron, for your continued support through my healing process and into the sharing of my story.

Thank you to the Star Teachings Community, for helping me to share my story and to write an even better story for the future. Thank you for your kindness, compassion, and happiness.

To all of you who supported and backed this book during my Kickstarter campaign. I couldn't have done this without you! Thank you for your incredible support!

About the Author

Jaclyn Ouillette Sanipass has a B.A. in Outdoor Education & Wilderness Leadership. Following a devastating battle with Lyme disease, she recovered and led Women's Wilderness Retreats for over 10 years—achieving what the doctors said was impossible. She is a survivor in complete recovery from severe neurologic Lyme disease. Jaclyn currently resides in Maine with her husband and daughter and enjoys traveling the world speaking and teaching.

Find our more about Jaclyn on her website
www.JaclynSanipass.com

Can You Help?

Thank You So Much For Reading My Book!

I appreciate all of your feedback, and I
love hearing your thoughts.

I need your input to make the next version of
this book and my future books even better.

Please leave me an honest review on Amazon
letting me know what you thought of the book.

Thank You So Much!

Jaclyn Ouillette Sanipass

Next Steps

For Writings, Inspirations, Books, & Jewelry
Visit Jaclyn's website www.JaclynSanipass.com

To Book Jaclyn for Speaking, Teachings, or Workshops
info@jaclynsanipass.com

Watch for Jaclyn's next books coming soon!
The Book of TEA'S
The Secret Book of the Dragon

For Information on Sho-Kai
www.collegeofshokai.org

For Sound Journeys, TEA'S, Ancient Teachings & More
www.ancientechoes.org

Made in the USA
Monee, IL
20 March 2021

63338955R00146